Free At Last!

The Past May Look Dismal
But The Future Is Bright!

Nancy A. Rockey, Ph.D. & Ron Rockey, Ph.D.

Published by eBookIt.com

ISBN-13: 978-1-4566-1759-2

Acknowledgments

There have been so many people—family, friends, colleagues and clients alike—who have contributed to this book in various ways.

Our family has endured long silences as we dedicated ourselves to researching, writing and re-writing the contents of this book. Colleagues have given their opinions and, more importantly, their support and encouragement for the project. Clients have even sacrificed appointments so that we could persevere in its writing in order to meet our deadlines. Our friends have listened and read, asked for clarity, supported our efforts with "around the house" assistance, and also prayed for the completion of this project and the benefit to those who read and apply to themselves the information contained herein.

Priscilla S. Perry, our longtime friend and colleague, has spent hours editing, placing and replacing commas, and suggesting sentence re-writes. Her dear husband, Don, has no doubt had to wait for meals and miss out on conversation time with his wife. You two have been a constant blessing during this project, and precious friends for so many years—1960, wasn't it?

And to those whose stories we have told, many of whom will recognize the story but not the name given to the character— we are grateful! Your paths to wholeness provide the interesting examples of what can occur in life when people are given the right information, a safe place for learning and change, and the power of the Holy Spirit.

Dedication

This book is whole-heartedly dedicated
to all who ever felt imprisoned by rejection,
whether it was in a fleeting moment
or every day of your lives.
Our prayer is that this study will allow
you to look within yourself in an
in-depth manner and do the work of
recovery, so that you can be
Free At Last!
And to every person whose tender
heart prompts them to
walk alongside.

"A human being is a part of a whole . . . (but) he experiences himself, his thoughts and feelings as something separated from the rest . . . This delusion is a kind of prison for us, restricting us to our personal desires and to affection for a few persons nearest to us. Our task must be to free ourselves from this prison by widening our circle of compassion to embrace all living creatures and the whole of nature in its beauty."

Albert Einstein

Table of Contents

Preface

Many of us have wondered why we find ourselves in such a mess, why we do the things we do, why our thoughts run amuck, why we are judgmental and critical of others, why it's easy to put others down and lift ourselves up. Sometimes we even chatter to ourselves asking, "How could I be so stupid? What in the world was I thinking?" Or we pat ourselves on the back, considering that the thoughts running through our heads are clever paybacks to someone we believe has "done it to us."

Where do these thoughts come from anyway? Is there a reason for them? And what about our behaviors? Do you ever find yourself blowing up at someone and then, later, unable to fathom why you've done it? Do you have some addictive behavior or persistent thoughts that you just can't shake, and wonder why the tug is so powerful? Do you struggle with thinking that you have value or worth, and can quickly manufacture a list of what's wrong with you? Do you cover up the negative way you think of yourself with an air of sophistication—"I've got it all together"—or arrogance, repeated laughter at almost every sentence you utter, or anger that's out of control? Do you long for a close relationship or two, but the minute someone accepts and seems to love you, you push them away?

There are answers; there are reasons for your feelings, thoughts and behaviors. People don't just wake up one morning and "out of the blue" decide that this is the day they will rob a bank or take someone's life or throw a temper tantrum. There is always a beginning, always a set-up, and in most cases the set-up started years before the thoughts and actions began. Mind you, there is never an excuse, because **an excuse is simply a cover-up.** But there is ALWAYS a reason, and **a reason is a set-up.**

So what is it that sets a person up to be offensive? Could it be some life experience(s)? Many are trapped in the prison houses of their minds, while others wind up behind brick walls because they were caught.

Are the stories of our histories just excuses, cover-ups, for evil people with evil motives to do as they please?

Introduction

The question is asked, "Where do our thoughts and feelings and behaviors come from?" How is it that we find ourselves in situations that just should not have occurred? Is it possible to change the way we feel, our thinking patterns and even the behaviors that sever us from relationships that we had cherished and even needed? Is it helpful to blame others for the way we are, or is it better to bury our heads in the sand, so to speak, and pretend that we are OK, and it's the world that's all wrong?

Regardless of where you might find yourself in life, please know that there has always been a set-up; there has always been some previous experience(s) that set you on a path to where you are, positive or negative. Understanding the cause of your feelings, thoughts and behaviors, and being willing to work through those negative experiences, can give you the power and permission to remove the negative emotions from your memories, thus eliminating the negative results in your life. It can provide you with gratitude toward those who contributed to your successes and the wisdom to recognize that all of your experiences have made you who you are.

If you find yourself on a negative pathway with your relationships crumbling, addictions controlling you, angry or tearful outbursts occurring at the drop of a hat, the inability to hold onto a career or job, being repeatedly in trouble with the law or incarcerated, your physical health diminishing, living with a "poor me" or negative mindset, and blaming everyone else and everything else for your predicaments, this book is for you.

Perhaps you are a parent, a close relative, a pastor, or someone just trying to help someone whose life is going in the wrong direction to turn around. You might find yourself in the position where you just don't know what to do, and because you are a religious person you think that convincing that person to read the Bible, follow God, pray, or subscribe to a certain religion will do the trick. Inevitably, you will be disappointed with the outcome.

You see, the truth is that God is ALWAYS the power for positive change and for turning a life around, but there is also always an obstacle to being able to clearly see the light of God's goodness and mercy as well as His ability and desire to transform a life. That obstacle creates a shadow, and most often we live in the shadow of that obstacle. Removing the obstacle, taking the negativity away from the obstacle and the experiences of life that create the shadow, allows us to see the light of God's goodness and turn life toward a relationship with Him.

If you just want to understand where you are, how you got there, and how you can make positive changes in your life, this book is also for you. If you find yourself alone and lonely, and wish that someone understood your plight and could be the confidant that you need, you just may find your solutions here. Let's begin at life's beginnings and discover how all of mankind has been set up—how, as individuals, we can move toward peace, joy, love and change, from **covering up** to **fessing up** and **living up** to the full potential that we were created to experience.

Chapter One

The Set-Up

In the very beginning of mankind, we started off on the wrong foot! We wanted more than what we had. Selfishness became the norm for mankind, and relationships with others became problematic. You know how it is, don't you? We are still like that today. If there's something within view of us, something that is or isn't good for us, we want it if it catches our eye and tickles our fancy. We tend to have the hardest time staying away from what we know we shouldn't have because it will hurt us. We just have to try it, even if it's taboo. To children, if the forbidden "do not touch" looks attractive, they long to get the object in their hands. And once we have what we desire, we have to have more, and there we go down the path toward self-pleasing and narcissism.

The set-up for our continued suffering occurred at the beginning of time and continues its trek down through time in each generation and in every family. Our genes carry within them the characteristics of the generations before us—at least four generations prior to ours. Our environment from conception onward, combined with those genes we inherited, determines who we are, how we tend to think and feel, and, most definitely, how we behave. And our genes have been, according to fairly new science, designed to be changed. Several important ingredients combine to facilitate change.

EARLY INFLUENCES

The latest scientific research, combined with years of the study of mankind, has determined that who you become is greatly influenced by your time in your mother's womb. But even what science has assumed for years—that we are not changeable or fixable—has been turned on its heels by new science. New science assures us that we are changeable and fixable. There is hope for us if we want to change and become emotionally un-chained from the negative influences of our beginnings.

From the moment of conception and until you were born, you were increasingly influenced by what went on around you in the womb. Your mother's health, her stress level, sounds in her environment, her ability to connect with you as you grew and developed, and her hormone levels all had an impact on your development. Believe it or not, according to Dr. Thomas Verny, a child psychiatrist and pediatrician who has researched the womb environment for a number of years, "the most impactful influence on a developing child in the womb is the relationship between a pregnant mother and the man who impregnated her." If that relationship is ended, if he did not want her to carry through with the pregnancy, or if he is absent or abusive, those conditions would negatively impact the child as it developed in the womb. Just remember, though: It's all fixable. It's not fix-able by changing the past—that is impossible! But what IS possible is changing the negative emotions you may keep in-side you for nearly a lifetime. If you are teachable, you are fix-able!

Adrenaline, noradrenaline and cortisol, hormones that are nec-essary for us to react properly in an emergency, are also pro-duced in stress. But when produced in a larger than normal amount in a pregnant woman, they can cause abnormal connec-tions between the neurons in the brain of a fetus. The hormones travel from the mother to the fetus via her placenta. This does not mean that the baby will necessarily be abnormal, but it may be hypervigilant and overly sensitive, especially to perceived rejection.

Another effect that has bearing on you results if your delivery or process of being born was a difficult one. Adding to the physical difficulty of a complicated birth would be the absence of your birth father during your delivery. Birth complications include but aren't limited to:

- Cesarean section

- Premature birth

- Emergency delivery due to hemorrhage from placenta previa or abruption

- Baby in distress (abnormally low or high heart rate)

- Breech or transverse position of baby in the uterus

- Use of forceps or suction cup to pull baby out of the birth canal

- Mother's health compromised due to bleeding or high blood pressure

Add to the above the inability of your mother to bond with you emotionally. There is a list of reasons why she might not have been able to bond, such as:

- The way her own parents did or did not bond with her

- Her relationship with your birth father (absent or abusive)

- Pregnancy came at an inconvenient time

- Conception took place outside of marriage

- You were of the wrong sex, so your birth displeased her

- You looked like your father or someone from his side of the family, from which she was alienated

- You reminded her of someone on her side that she disliked

- She was upset by the change in her figure

The list of reasons goes on and on, but the most likely is that she was not well attached to her own parents and therefore lacked both the knowledge and the experience of bonding with a child.

RON'S STORY

Ron was an unwanted child! Though his mother and father were fairly stable, they did not want and couldn't afford a fourth child; so every attempt had been made to end this pregnancy, without success.

Butch, as they nicknamed him when they saw his size, was born in his parent's attic. He was a ten-and-a-half-pound bouncer at birth, and the difficult delivery took a devastating toll on his mother. Immediately she was rushed off to the hospital, as the birth had torn internal organs; and without repair she would have died.

Her hospital stay was lengthy, and for some time there was talk amongst family members that she would never return home, as the birth experience had forced her near to death. No one was left to care for Butch except his older siblings. His nine-year-old sister, Phyllis, took on the responsibility of mothering him as best a nine-year-old could. His father was working a job four hours away from home. It was wartime, and Stanley was doing the heating and air-conditioning for ships that were destined for the battle overseas. During the day, while Phyllis and the two other siblings were in school, a 16-year-old neighbor was Butch's babysitter.

When Renata was finally released from the hospital, Stanley took her to be with him while he worked in the shipyards. Occasionally they would come home for a few days, and little Butch became acquainted with his parents briefly, until they left again.

The world-famous British psychologist Dr. John Bowlby, with the help of a man named James Robertson, identified three stages of separation response amongst children:

> **Protest** *to the mother figure for re-attachment (related to separation anxiety). This is when the child cries, screams, rattles the crib sides, jumps up and down, repeatedly calls*

"Mommy." This demonstrates the child's anger at being left behind and the attempt to get the mother to return for him. Finally when the cries do not gain the desired response, the child will go to Stage 2.

Despair *and pain at the loss of the mother figure despite repeated protests for re-establishment for relationship (related to grief and mourning). During this period the child pouts, whimpers quietly, seems distant, is inclined to not eat or drink nor play. Again this period can last from a day to weeks, depending on the child.*

Detachment *or denial of affection to the mother figure.*

These phases are universally seen in children who go through separation, either by loss of parent/s due to death, divorce or through boarding school. Bowlby identified that infants need one special relationship for internal development.

No variables have more far-reaching effects on personality development than a child's experiences within the family. Starting during his first months in his relation to both parents, he builds up working models of how attachment figures are likely to behave towards him in any of a variety of situations, and on all those models are based all his expectations, and therefore all his plans, for the rest of his life.

Maternal Care and Mental Health, New York: Scocken Books, 1966. Page 369.

Being an unwanted child, having had attempts made on his life while in the womb, having an absent and angry father, and being raised during the most important years of his life (the first two) by children—all these things gave Butch not only the sense but also the knowledge that he did not belong. He lived and felt like an orphan in his own family, even when the war was over and his parents finally returned home. As far as he was concerned, his sister Phyllis was the closest to him and a substitute mother.

When he was four, his birth mother would give him a quarter and send him off by himself to the movies. That quarter would buy him two full-length movies and the cartoon and news reels in between. He could even squeeze out a bag of popcorn with that money. Those twenty-five-cent pieces meant, to Butch, "Be gone a long time!" And so he quickly became a loner. The two friends he did have during those early years (from birth to seven) both died—one of hemophilia and the other of complications from polio.

One day, when he was about six years old, he came home from the movies to find a baby in a cradle in his parents' bedroom. This was a new brother, Bobby. His mother's attitude and behavior toward Bobby were totally foreign to him. "What is with all this hugging, kissing and rocking?" he wondered. As the months went by, he felt further distanced from Renata and detected his mother's preference for and adoration of his little brother. Butch chose to be absent from the house as much as possible. The feelings he had been experiencing all his life had been confirmed: "I am not wanted, I am not loved, I might as well cut myself off from these people and just take care of myself."

Meanwhile, his brother George, who was eight years older than him, had become the family scapegoat. George was beaten regularly down in the basement furnace room with Dad's leather strap. His mother would sit on the cellar steps and egg Daddy on to beat George harder and longer for the misdoings of all the kids and for things for which he'd already been beaten. Butch shared a room with George, and his brother would often come to bed beaten, bruised, blistered and bleeding, and would rock in his bunk trying to comfort himself from the injustice he had received. His older sisters would come and beat George on the head with their high-heeled shoes in an endeavor to shut him up. Ron got a strong message from those experiences: "Trust no one, especially women, 'cuz they will betray you!" And George, well, his life is quite another story!!

By the time Ron was sixteen, he had endured unjust punishments too, but not the beatings like George. When asked about it, Dad said he was just trying to beat good sense into George, and it wasn't working. So with Butch, he did the opposite—no touch, no connection, no inclusion and no love. Discouraged and struggling with learning at school, he quit high school after the ninth grade and went to work.

On Halloween night, Stanley went out with an old sheet over his head to play ghost for the neighborhood kids as they came across the bridge that crossed over a little brook. He came home rather late and was pretty tired, and Butch was already asleep. Soon Butch was shaken out of a sound sleep. "Come now—Dad is dying!" his sisters screamed. You see, Butch had joined the Boy Scouts and had worked his way up to an Eagle Scout. It was there that he learned mouth-to-mouth resuscitation and cardiac massage. With Dad in his arms, he struggled to do both, but to no avail. His Dad died in his arms. At that moment the message was imprinted: "No matter what I do, no matter how hard I try, it's never good enough. I will never get it right enough to be accepted."

The next morning, Ron bought a newspaper and went to the bridge that spanned the Arkansas River. In his hiding place under the bridge, he read his father's obituary. That day he made what he called "a deal with God." He said, "God, you take my Dad to heaven, and I'll take his place in hell." And, as he tells it, he came out from beneath that bridge with the determination to go straight to hell, whatever it took.

Of course, it was not that he hadn't already done some illegal and mischievous things. By that time he had already determined that if the world, including his family, wouldn't give him what he needed, then he would just take what he wanted, regardless of who owned it. He had been sexually abused numerous times by older boys and men, and the rage that came from those experiences added to his need to take what he wanted became the formula for a downward spiral to prison.

At seventeen he finally landed in juvenile court and was given the option: join the armed forces or face juvenile detention. Ron joined the Navy. He soon discovered that no one was cuddling and loving him there, so he continued his crime spree, taking what he wanted. Mostly he wanted liquor, because it helped to dull the pain in his heart from years of not belonging or being loved. After two years in the Navy and a devastating fall from a high point on a ship, he was honorably discharged from the service, narrowly escaping a general court-martial.

As is often the case, one thing led to another; habits are formed easily and hard to break, especially when they are fueled by perceived injustice and boiling anger. So his crime continued landing him in one prison after another, one from which he escaped. He later paid the time for that in Tennessee's Big House in Nashville. The movies *The Green Mile* and *The Last Castle* were both filmed at that prison. Angry and still alone, he felt that life was really not worth living, especially considering that his future at that hellish prison was bleak.

Rejection, which is what he felt from his family, is extremely difficult for those who have experienced it. It gives the victim the idea that their worth and value are minimal at best, and anger seethes within. Especially hard for a boy is rejection experienced from his mother, as it sets in place a mindset that all women are suspect. While he grows up longing to be in intimate relationships with women, those relationships are often unsuccessful. Actually believing that he is loved by a woman, any woman, is difficult because of the original non-acceptance by his mother. Everything the woman does is scrutinized, every action she takes is questioned, and every phone call she makes is a reason to accuse her of betraying him. Often this is the beginning of domestic violence.

The God-given software, already programmed in the human brain, is that we are to honor our mothers and fathers. When a fellow, for whatever reason, has built up resentment toward his mother, he often takes out that anger and frustration on his wife. The rage that comes from not being able to alter his relationship with his mother is dumped onto his unsuspecting wife. He may restrain, pinch, beat, or otherwise physically or sexually abuse his wife, not because of real anger at her but rather out of frustration with his mother. Ron lived with that negative mindset for years during his nearly-50-year marriage with Nancy, and of course it was a cause of great marital difficulty! By the grace of God, physical abuse never occurred, but it is still possible to do significant damage with spoken words. It took a determined plan for him to recover from his original childhood wounds and to begin erasing the pain that he carried. He feared that at some point Nancy would leave him—either for another man, or in sickness or death. "After all, if my mother who bore me didn't love me, why should a strange woman who comes into my life?" He asked that question of himself repeatedly.

From his childhood onward, Ron took with him everywhere he went the feeling that he was unloved and unwanted, and didn't belong. The story of his prison years is written in a book entitled *Chosen*, which is unfortunately now out of print. (It is occasionally available on Amazon.com) That feeling showed up in every relationship and in every endeavor of his life. Sheer determination, along with the gift of direction from God, helped him to overcome. We will look at what became of him and his life later in this book.

> *The view that maternal deprivation has dire effects on personality gained support from case histories documenting maternal rejection in the backgrounds of aggressive youngsters and from studies of children reared in orphanages, many of whom became delinquents. Indeed, John Bowlby suggested that the discovery of a need for maternal affection during early childhood paralleled the discovery of the role of vitamins in physical health.*

John Bowlby, *Maternal Care and Mental Health*. Page 59.

Just as the physical body lacking the proper nutrients for health will develop disease, so the child's brain lacking physical affection, especially from the mother, will develop tendencies toward criminality.

> *Using multiple sources for information about parent-child relations, Sheldon and Eleanor Glueck found that parental rejection was a strong predictor of criminality. After coding case records based on home observations for a period of approximately five years, Joan McCord retraced 235 members of the Cambridge Somerville Youth Study. She found that those who had mothers who were self-confident, provided leadership, were consistently non-punitive, and affectionate were unlikely to commit crimes. Thus, studies on emotional climate in the home present consistent results. Like parental conflict, negative parent-child relations enhance the probability of delinquency. Parental affection appears to reduce the probability of crime. Not surprisingly, parental affection and close family ties tend to be linked with other features of family interaction.*

Sheldon Glueck and Eleanor T. Glueck, *Unraveling Juvenile Delinquency*. New York: Commonwealth Fund, 1950.

Most of the responses to rejection are self-destructive. The torture of keeping a mental list of abuses only piles on the resentment and bitterness as the list increases in length. Emotional paralysis seems to take over, but eventually an explosion of catastrophic dimensions will occur, with the fallout landing either on oneself or on those with whom the victim is closest. Retaining slights or purposeful rejections, which one cannot help but do because they are emotionally charged, constructs a set of grey, cloudy glasses worn every day by the victim and used to predict and prevent reactions from all they meet. Why should this be? It is because the brain has a method of working, a design to help us protect ourselves and have the ammunition to combat further rejections. The only issue here is that those attacks keep piling up and eventually can cause volcanic-type eruptions when we least expect them. Furthermore, those reactions and eruptions bring to us the very rejection that we fear.

Alice Miller, a widely-published and well-known author, has achieved worldwide recognition for her work on the causes and effects of child abuse and its cost to society. In her book entitled *The Drama of Being a Child,* first published in 1987 and revised in 1995, she states:

> *Experience has taught us that we have only one enduring weapon in our struggle against mental illness: the emotional discovery of the truth about the unique history of our childhood.*

She continues:

> *The truth is so essential that its loss exacts a heavy toll, in the form of grave illness. In order to become whole we must try, in a long process, to discover our own personal truth, a truth that may cause pain before giving us a new sphere of freedom. If we choose instead to content ourselves with intellectual "wisdom," we will remain in the sphere of illusion and self-deception.*

> Pages 1-2.

Powerful words, aren't they? But oh so true! There is always a precipitating event producing inhibitions and fear, but it is possible to break through the shadow of the past and into the light of accomplishment, success and emotional growth. Interest in the subject of rejection is, therefore, a path of wisdom. Physical, emotional and spiritual health will greatly benefit from the decision to honestly face one's feelings head on. The ways that we connect or plug in to each other are greatly influenced by the shadows created from our early experiences of attaching to primary caregivers in childhood. That attachment is determined by how those parents or primary caregivers were equipped to bond with us. Because our need to survive is so strong, it has determined how or if we will attach to others in our lives in a secure manner. Our ability to attach or to plug in has also been impacted by the wounds we received while we were in the process of determining our worth and value. (The first two years of life are the most impactful, but up to age seven is when our thoughts and feelings are formed.) Let's face it, the bottom line is this: *Wounded people wound people.* Rejected people look for rejection under every rock, and nearly always find it. If they do not find it, they create it by behaving in such a manner that others will reject them. Their shadow enlarges in the process.

After half a century of studying parental rejection and acceptance, Dr. Ronald Rohner of the University of Connecticut's Family Studies Department has concluded that if a person *perceives* he is rejected, he has received it. One's perception is one's reality.

So, if during your character-forming years (conception through age seven) you felt like you did not belong among your family or friends, or if you currently find yourself being sensitive to the slights of others and predicting that your friends or family will reject you, you will find your answers here! Be careful in scrutinizing yourself, because it is easy to fool ourselves with cover-ups that we have devised in an attempt to look strong. There is so much more to learn and apply to yourself about the influence of rejection on a life.

Chapter Two

Rejection And Anger

Until his death, Dr. John Joseph Evoy was an expert in the ins and outs of rejection. In fact, he would see in his practice only those who reported that rejection was in their experience. His famous book entitled *The Rejected* has been a blessing to many for detailing the remnants of early rejection during childhood and adolescence.

> *The greatest terror a child can have is that he is not loved, and rejection is the hell he fears. I think that everyone in the world to a large or small extent has felt rejection. And with rejection comes anger, and with anger some kind of crime in revenge for the rejection, and with the crime—guilt—and there is the story of mankind.*

The Rejected by Dr. John Joseph Evoy. Page 10.

Furthermore, his book is packed with information about the anger, fears, anxieties, guilt and depression, and the behaviors they produce, in rejected individuals. To copy all of his information would basically call for a complete re-write of his research and that of the other experts he cites. Since that is impossible in this book, we will instead highlight some of his written information and provide charts in an attempt to synthesize this valuable material in an easily understood and more concise fashion. We will quote some of his main points first and then present them in graphic form for ease of understanding.

Anger that is displayed in those who have been rejected stems from a sense of being unjustly treated. Parents who have neglected, demeaned, ignored, or physically or sexually abused their children, who simply need love as much as they need food, air and water, appear to be the cause.

Certainly, that was the case with Ron, whose story is in Chapter One. The ignoring and neglect was most painful for him when his baby brother was brought home from the hospital. It was then that he saw preferential treatment toward the younger brother. The hugging and the kissing, the rocking and the tender care of his adoring mother had been totally absent from Ron's experience. Why wouldn't a little boy think that he'd been treated unfairly and unjustly? Why wouldn't he be angry? Why wouldn't he direct some of that anger toward himself and keep it hidden inside until he couldn't bear it any longer? So the boy (Ron) became a loner and spent many hours away from home because he believed that he was unwanted and unloved. The idea that "something must be wrong with me" is what he as a child would come to believe, considering the circumstances. Here is the beginning of his diminishing self-concept; here is the continuing sense that he doesn't really belong in his family. Here is the beginning of a determination to make it on his own—to do it himself, regardless of what it would take.

In a tiny book entitled *By God's Grace, Sam*, the story of Sam's life is told.

Samuel Woodrow Tannyhill was born to parents who seemed to adore him, but they couldn't get along with each other. Their divorce took place when he was only five years old, but divorces don't happen suddenly. There is usually tension in the relationship and an inability to get along with each other long before a marriage ends. While a child might not be able to recall his parents' relationship from when he was an infant or a toddler, the atmosphere around each of his parents, and in the home, dramatically impacts the child.

A child below the age of three isn't able to readily distinguish between himself and his parents, so he takes responsibility for what is happening between the parents. He tries in his own little ways to fix the parents, but cannot. He then sees himself as a failure. Of course, he doesn't necessarily have the language to express that he thinks he has failed, but the feelings of failure and not being good enough are still strong within him.

SAM'S STORY

As a boy, Sam could never look back on a pleasant, happy childhood such as most boys enjoy. Both of his parents thought a great deal of him, but when he was five years old, they separated. These circumstances cast the little fellow adrift among relatives and friends who offered to take care of him.

Growing up maladjusted and starved for affection, Sam lived in a dozen different homes in the next few years. Looking back on what this experience did to him, various members of his family wished they might have realized his need and given him a permanent home in their family groups.

By the time realization arrived, it was already too late. In some of the homes where Sam lived he was treated almost cruelly by those who thought they were teaching him obedience, but whose methods could do nothing but arouse his resentment.

When Sam was in his early teens, his father, ill with a heart condition, invited Sam to make his home with him. By that time Sam was associating with a very rough crowd, and frequently would be gone till all hours of the night and early morning. His father would lie on his bed and worry about where his boy might be. Even though he was unable to get around very well, he would laboriously get out of bed to go out and walk up and down the streets, trying to catch a glimpse of his son. This good and wholesome influence was cut short by the death of his father when Sam was only fifteen. Once again he was set adrift, and his life of crime continued to develop.

Because of Sam's insecurity in childhood, his schoolwork suffered accordingly. Although he had a brilliant mind, he never satisfactorily completed a single grade in school. Al-

ways he was passed on to the next grade even though he had not applied himself to his lessons. When he reached the sixth grade his formal schooling came to an end. This limited schooling showed up in his spelling and occasional grammatical errors.

Sam's criminal life began at the age of ten or eleven, when he had his first brush with the law. It was felt at that time that this incident was not very important, and no one was too concerned about it. It was agreed that surely he would outgrow any antisocial tendencies that were then displayed. As a result, nothing was done to guide him along better lines. He was given no moral training and never stepped foot inside a church in all his life.

Pages 7-8.

Let's go back and take a look at what we have learned about Sam so far.

Supposedly, Sam's first five years were wonderful, and he was cared for by loving parents. Considering the fact that a divorce occurred between his parents when he was five, there had to have been tension in his home—tension that was profound, obvious, and experienced by the child. You might ask, does a child really comprehend and feel this tension? The answer is a shocking YES. We know that children are very sensitive, some even more so than others. Their young behaviors demonstrate what is going on in the home. Excessive crying, a tendency to be frequently angry, throwing toys around, and even attempting to bite, slap, or kick their parents are all signs of stress.

In an article by Dr. Bruce D. Perry, a child psychiatrist who founded the Child Trauma Academy in 1990, he states:

Studies of childhood abuse and neglect have important lessons for considerations of nature and nurture. While each child has unique genetic potentials, both human and animal studies point to important needs that every child has, and severe long-term consequences for brain function if those needs are not met. The effects of the childhood environment, favorable or unfavorable, interact with all the processes of neurodevelopment.

Abuse studies from the author's laboratory, studies of children in orphanages who lacked emotional contact, and a large number of animal deprivation and enrichment studies point to the need for children and young nonhuman mammals to have both stable emotional attachments with and touch from primary adult caregivers, and spontaneous interactions with peers. If these connections are lacking, brain development both of caring behavior and cognitive capacities is damaged in a lasting fashion [regardless of the reasons for deprivation].

"Childhood Experience and the Expression of Genetic Potential: What Childhood Neglect Tells Us About Nature and Nurture."

In Dr. Perry's book *The Boy Who Was Raised As A Dog*, he states:

Traumatized children tend to have overactive stress responses and . . . these can make them aggressive, impulsive and needy. These children are difficult, they are easy to upset and hard to calm, they may overreact to the slightest novelty or change and they often don't know how to think before they act. Before they can make any kind of lasting change at all in their behavior, they need to feel safe and loved.

It appears, therefore, that from a very early age, both psychological and physiological damage can occur from abuse, neglect, or extended illness on the part of parent or child—illness that causes separation. Remember that even a difficult birth has its consequences.

Let's ask these questions:

Where was Sam's father after the divorce? Nothing is said of his father until the boy was an early teenager, and certainly by that point the absence of a father figure had already warped or distorted his thinking. His model for manhood had disappeared at age five and was replaced with various other negative models until he got his father back years later. What did he learn from other father figures? It would appear that what he learned encouraged him down the path of early criminal behaviors. The damage had already been done to this boy, such that only a personal understanding of his beginnings and a willingness to look at them and to forgive the perpetrators would begin the process of self-understanding and change.

Dr. Perry states in his book *Born to Love*:

> . . . *I have found that there are complex interactions beginning in early childhood that affect our ability to envision choices and that may later limit our ability to make the best decisions.*

You will see the truth of Dr. Perry's statement as Sam's story continues.

Where was Sam's mother after the divorce? Did you notice that nothing is said of her at all? While a boy's father is important as a model for manhood, his mother is necessary for the tender love and affection that eventually he should look for in the woman he marries. It is definitely true that a mother is primary in a boy's young life as a compassionate, concerned caregiver. If she just disappeared after the divorce, poor Sam was left wondering what he did so wrong that Mom would abandon him. Dad's work should have been that of provider, protector and priest, and he abdicated that role until the boy was a teen.

During the years after his parents' divorce, Sam was bounced around from one home to another, and in each place he lived he suffered. Sam endured eight lost years without either parent, years filled with abuse, mistreatment, and more abandonment. Those essential years of character formation and elementary education were years of absolute torture and self-punishment. He was dumbed down by the abuse he received in his multiple foster homes, and he sabotaged his own educational success because of it.

When there is no security, no consistency in a child's experience, he flounders like a ship on the sea without a compass and no land in sight. His reference points are missing, his goals are non-existent, as he wanders from day to day in an attempt to find a safe harbor.

Does it sound like we are making excuses for his behaviors here? Remember, *excuses are cover-ups*, and what we are doing is exposing the *real* truth about Sam's beginnings. We are giving *reasons* for the devastation of his subsequent years.

In Dr. Perry's book *Born to Love*, we read:

> . . . *early experiences will necessarily have a far greater impact than later ones. The brain tries to make sense of the world by looking for patterns. When it links coherent, consistently connected patterns together, it tags them as "normal" or "expected" and stops paying attention. So for example, the very first time you were placed in a sitting position as an infant, you did pay attention to the novel sensations emanating from your buttocks. Your brain learned to sense the pressure associated with sitting normally, you began to sense how to balance your weight to sit upright via your motor vestibular system and, eventually you learned to sit.*

Page 29.

Dr. Perry instructs that, to the neurons and neural systems of the brain, patterns of experience matter.

> *On a cell by cell basis, no other tissue* (other than the brain) *is more suited to change in response to patterned, repetitive signals.*

Page 29.

Dr. Perry concurs with the work of Seymour Levine, who postulates that children are more vulnerable to trauma than adults.

The developing brain is most malleable (impressionable) and most sensitive to experiences—good and bad—that occur early in life. Because of this, **we are also rapidly and easily transformed by trauma when we are young.**

Learning patterns came early for Sam with the loss of both parents. Being bounced between family and friends for the next eight or so years exaggerated the pattern already established, and over and over again it was fortified with each subsequent move from one family to another. Adding to the pattern was the abuse. Wouldn't you think that the pattern he learned might in time impact the family of his own that he might endeavor to establish later in life? We'll look at that as his story continues.

We know for sure that children who are abused are either dumbed down by the abuse or become so depressed and feel so worthless that their schoolwork suffers. Sam is referenced as having a brilliant mind, but often those with the brilliant minds are behavior problems in school. Why? They have a hard time sitting still and focusing on the project at hand because their minds are occupied with an overabundance of ideas running constantly through their heads. Their bodies attempt to keep up with the busyness of their minds by moving about and being disruptive rather than sitting quietly at their desks. The methods of learning used in the school systems do not make sense to many of these bright ones, and they become frustrated as they endeavor to learn by the left-brain methods of their teachers. Often they give up, just as Sam and Ron did.

As if Sam hadn't endured enough tragedy and loss, another loss occurred when he was 15, after nearly three years of living with his seriously ill birth father. Even though, at the time he moved into his father's house, he had already been three years into crime, there had to have been moments when he felt his father's love and concern. When Sam would stay out late and into the wee hours of the morning, his father would get out of bed and walk the streets hoping to catch a glimpse of his son. That must have felt good to Sam—to know that someone actually cared. When Sam was 15, his father died, and once again he was out on the streets, alone and unloved and adrift.

During the few years after he quit school in grade six, Sam stole six cars, and he was caught twice. Deciding that stealing cars wasn't such a great idea, he began forging checks, but he kept being caught. The police were also putting pressure on him for not being in school.

Jumping from job to job quickly became tiring, so Sam enlisted in the Army. After a very brief stint in the Army, Sam decided that military life wasn't for him. He continued to steal and forge checks while in the Army, which got him relocated from his original base five times before the Army finally discharged him.

Once out of military service, he met a girl and got married; but in two months he tired of her and left her. A few months later, he met another girl. *"She was a good girl,"* he said, *"and she couldn't understand why they had to keep moving around so much."* Finally he got a job driving a dump truck, but one night he decided to *"clean out a grocery store."* Things became intense then with "the law," but still he kept on with his robberies.

His wife wanted to move back to her hometown, as she was about to have a baby. On the way there, Sam was stopped for speeding. The law then caught up with him for previous infractions, and he was sentenced to seven years in jail.

Somehow his wife managed to get him parole in 17 months. He soon became tired of his parole officer, and he took off again, leaving his newly pregnant wife and child with her grandparents. He was divorced after his second child was born. Quite a pattern of instability, wouldn't you say? And what you have read so far is minus many of the details of his criminal life.

After getting out of prison in Missouri, he went to see his mother. This is the first time we have heard of her since his parents' divorce! He stayed with her for one week and then headed for Indianapolis. There he worked days and cashed checks at night, and he also pulled two robberies. After a couple of weeks, he headed back home and decided to pull off one more job and then head out of town with his new girlfriend. Do you notice how Sam kept moving around from one woman to another? Was he looking for a wife to mother him, since his years of "mothering" had been abruptly ended when his parents divorced? Would any woman be good enough, do it right, or condone his unlawfulness?

This "one more" job was a robbery of a restaurant where only one waitress worked the night shift. He pointed his gun at her and emptied the cash register, but he was afraid to just leave because she could identify him. So he forced her into his car, planning to drive her several miles away so she would have to walk back to the restaurant, which would take her several hours. Sam thought that this would give him enough time to pick up his girlfriend and be way out of town by the time the authorities were called.

Things don't always go as planned, however, and that night Sam's plans went awry. The waitress recognized him because she was a friend of Sam's sister. In the car she kept talking and threatening him, so Sam pulled over, dragged her out, took her down to a nearby creek, and bludgeoned her to death with a tire iron that had been on the floor in the back of his car. Her mutilated body was left there and found the next day. Talk about an explosion of rage! Sam must have felt a surge of rejection from her words of condemnation, and all that had happened since his birth added to what this waitress was saying. His anger blew over the top.

There had been a cab driver at the restaurant before the robbery. Sam had gone to the restaurant and waited for quite some time for the man to leave, but he lingered there, so Sam finally left. The cab driver was suspicious of Sam's intentions and wrote down his license plate number as Sam was leaving.

When the cabbie heard of the murder the next day, he called the police with the information.

Sam was pretty good at covering his tracks, and it was several weeks later, after Sam and his girlfriend had fled from his hometown and committed several armed robberies, that Sam was caught and connected to the waitress's murder.

> *In 1997, Joan McCord analyzed the effects of corporal punishment based on biweekly observation of 224 parents and their sons over an average period of five and one-half years. In addition to measuring the use of corporal punishment in the home, each parent was rated in terms of warmth expressed toward the child. At the time of these ratings, the sons were between the ages of ten and sixteen. Thirty years later, the criminal records of the subjects were traced. Regardless of whether or not a father was affectionate toward his son, his use of corporal punishment predicted an increased likelihood that the son would subsequently be convicted for a serious crime. Regardless of whether or not a mother was affectionate toward her son, the mother's use of corporal punishment predicted an increased likelihood that the son would subsequently be convicted for a serious violent crime.*
>
> Taken from the Encyclopedia of Crime and Justice, "Family Relationships and Crime." Joan McCord, 2002.

We know of Sam because his story was written in a little book entitled *By God's Grace, Sam*, which was written by a pastor who visited with Sam while he was in prison. The remainder of Sam's story, that of a rejected child who was abandoned, abused, and bounced around from place to place for years during his childhood and adolescence, is phenomenal, and will be told later. His story certainly verifies the fact that rejected individuals can easily become criminals as a reaction to their emotional pain. Remember, we are looking at *reasons*, not *excuses*.

Chapter Three

Rejection And Addictions

So far you have read about how experiences of early rejection have affected both Ron and Sam. The results of this trauma, and that of physical, sexual and emotional abuse, all of which are interpreted and reacted to as rejection, are far reaching.

Dr. Evoy reports, in his book, a statement by G. R. Hawkes:

> *The crux of parent-child relations as far as the child in the family is concerned, appears to be in the area of children's perceptions of what they, the parents, are, rather than in very definite and specific characteristics of home life.*

> *The Rejected.* Page 76.

According to Dr. Evoy, this means *that rejection is as it is experienced by the rejected person.* He continues:

> *A . . . consideration here is that there is a great deal of evidence to show that little children normally see their parents as ten-feet-high giants who are both omniscient and omnipotent. Accordingly, almost without exception, small children do not question the correctness of perceived parental evaluations and attitudes toward them, no matter how much they might dislike, resent, or be hurt by them. This correctness exists both at the child's intellectual and emotional levels.*

> Page 15.

Dr. Evoy's years of studies, and the studies of his peers, have established that children put their parents on pedestals of sorts, and basically worship them. They believe not only their parents' words and actions but also their attitudes. If parents' attitudes toward their children are not displayed in committed love, the children assume that they (the children) are at fault, not the parents.

Dr. Evoy continues:

Rejection . . . was not something these individuals happened to feel when they were depressed or otherwise out of sorts and which later disappeared when their spirits picked up. Rather, once they came to openly recognize the very painful feeling that they were rejected, it remained constant for them. Even when they happened not to be aware of it, the feeling of rejection did not go away. When not in the focus of their attention, it receded to the periphery of their awareness. Even successful psychotherapy did not phase out the hurts flowing from the experiences of rejection. It did, however, help the rejected to understand their rejection and cope more effectively with it.

Page 15.

RICK'S STORY

Ricky was his parents' firstborn son, and one would think that he would be the joy of their lives. One would assume that a father would be enthralled with his boy, his future football and baseball partner, a fishing buddy and a friend. But that was not to be Rick's experience. His mother was apparently overwhelmed with the care of a newborn and the simultaneous deterioration of her marriage. That joy that is necessary for a child to develop a positive worldview must have been absent between this mother and her baby. She was also unable to offer her son the kind of warmth and affection that a newborn or toddler needs. Unfortunately, her marital and subsequent divorce frustrations were dumped onto her defenseless boy. With a father who was not able to bond with his only son and a mother who could not give the maternal warmth and affection that Ricky needed, his parents must have come into marriage and parenthood with baggage of their own. We know now from scientific studies, which correspond to the word of God (see Exodus 20), that attitudes, behaviors, and physical attributes are passed on to the third and fourth generations.

When Ricky was two years old, his father finally left the family. At this point, Ricky's mother had to begin to work in order to support herself and her son, which escalated her feelings of frustration and anger. After a day at the office and the duties facing her when she got home, she was physically and emotionally spent. Often little Ricky, being a typical little boy, was active and would get into some minor trouble. A spilled glass of milk became his mother's excuse to beat him and yell obscenities at him. Over and over again, as Ricky grew, he was the object of her scorn.

A study conducted by E. F. Vogel and reported in his book *The Marital Relationship of Parents of Emotionally Disturbed Children: Polarization and Isolation* is recorded in Dr. Evoy's book, *The Rejected*, on page 402:

> *A common denominator in the study, however, was that . . . the children had felt they were not wanted and loved for themselves.*

Ricky's mother remarried a couple of years after her divorce from his father, and as a stranger joined the family, Ricky became the outsider. Of course, his mother's attention was focused toward her new husband, and the stepfather basically ignored the boy. Considering his mother's own emotional baggage, she married a man who was her emotional equal, so both then dumped their wounds, and the results of them, upon the boy. The truth is that, without recovery from the wounds of our pasts, we keep connecting with the same type of people over and over again. Why? Because, in most cases, we are endeavoring unconsciously to complete what was incomplete in our own histories. It would seem that, to Ricky's mother, a husband was far more important than a child. Ricky functioned as an addendum, not a focus.

Dr. Evoy describes rejection as *"their [child victims'] emotionally toned knowledge that they were not loved and wanted—for themselves—by one or both parents."*

So what does a kid do when he feels that he is basically not cared about or wanted? He or she becomes a loner. So, off by himself, Ricky did his own thing, occasionally getting into minor scrapes and suffering his mother's wrath at home.

Webster defines rejection as a "refusal to accept, receive, hear or consider important." In our book, *Belonging*, we define rejection as:

> *Rejection is a self-defeating feeling of hopelessness that comes from damages occurring during the prenatal and early childhood years. When the child's needs are not met, the child feels that he or she isn't important and, therefore, isn't worth very much. Experiences in later years compound the damage done when character is being forged in early childhood.*

Page 84.

At about age twelve, Ricky's mother sent him to spend a summer with his birth father, something that he hadn't done since his father had left when the boy was two years old. In the first place, Ricky's father was basically a stranger to him; and in the second, his father was not too thrilled about having the boy for the summer. Things didn't go very well. His father had remarried to a woman who had a couple of children herself, and they were a few years older than Rick. The older boys teased and tormented Rick incessantly. But the worst experience came when the stepbrothers sexually abused Rick. It wasn't so much the actual abuse that would torment Rick for years, although we know that male-to-male sexual abuse does create great anger in boys, sometimes even causing victims to question their own gender. The most merciless part of the events was that when Ricky told his father about them, there was a great upheaval. Not only did his father yell and scream, denying that the events had ever taken place (of course, the older boys denied it too), but, as a result, Dad packed up the boy's things and put him on a bus to return to his mother.

Male Sexual Victimization Myths & Facts

Adapted from a presentation at the 5th International Conference on Incest and Related Problems, Biel, Switzerland, August 14, 1991.

Myth #1—Boys and men can't be victims.

This myth, instilled through masculine gender socialization and sometimes referred to as the "macho image," declares that males, even young boys, are not supposed to be victims or even vulnerable. We learn very early that males should be able to protect themselves. In truth, boys are children—weaker and more vulnerable than their perpetrators—who cannot really fight back. Why? The perpetrator has greater size, strength, and knowledge. This power is exercised from a position of authority, using resources such as money or other bribes, or outright threats—whatever advantage can be taken to use a child for sexual purposes.

Myth #2—Most sexual abuse of boys is perpetrated by homosexual males.

Pedophiles who molest boys are not expressing a homosexual orientation any more than pedophiles who molest girls are practicing heterosexual behaviors. While many child molesters have gender and/or age preferences, of those who seek out boys, the vast majority are not homosexual. They are pedophiles.

Myth #3—If a boy experiences sexual arousal or orgasm from abuse, this means he was a willing participant or enjoyed it.

In reality, males can respond physically to stimulation (get an erection) even in traumatic or painful sexual situations. Therapists who work with sexual offenders know that one way a perpetrator can maintain secrecy is to label the child's sexual response as an indication of his willingness to participate. "You liked it, you wanted it," they'll say. Many survivors feel guilt and shame because they experienced physical arousal while being abused. Physical (and visual or auditory) stimulation is likely to happen in a sexual situation. It does not mean that the child wanted the experience or understood what it meant at the time.

Myth #4—Boys are less traumatized by the abuse experience than girls.

While some studies have found males to be less negatively affected, more studies show that long-term effects are quite damaging for either sex. Males may be more damaged by society's refusal or reluctance to accept their victimization, and by their resultant belief that they must "tough it out" in silence.

Myth #5—Boys abused by males are or will become homosexual.

While there are different theories about how the sexual orientation develops, experts in the human sexuality field do not believe that premature sexual experiences play a significant role in late adolescent or adult sexual orientation. It is unlikely that someone can make another person a homosexual or heterosexual. Sexual orientation is a complex issue and there is no single answer or theory that explains why someone identifies himself as homosexual, heterosexual or bisexual. Whether perpetrated by older males or females, boys' or girls' premature sexual experiences are damaging in many ways, including confusion about one's sexual identity and orientation.

Many boys who have been abused by males erroneously believe that something about them sexually attracts males, and that this may mean they are homosexual or effeminate. Again, not true. Pedophiles who are attracted to boys will admit that the lack of body hair and adult sexual features turns them on. The pedophile's inability to develop and maintain a healthy adult sexual relationship is the problem—not the physical features of a sexually immature boy.

Myth #6—The "Vampire Syndrome"—that is, boys who are sexually abused, like the victims of Count Dracula, go on to "bite" or sexually abuse others.

This myth is especially dangerous because it can create a terrible stigma for the child, namely, that he is destined to become an offender. Boys might be treated as potential perpetrators rather than victims who need help. While it is true that most perpetrators have histories of sexual abuse, it is NOT true that most victims go on to become perpetrators. Research by Jane Gilgun, Judith Becker, and John Hunter found a primary difference between perpetrators who were sexually abused and sexually abused males who never perpetrated: non-perpetrators told about the abuse, and were believed and supported by significant people in their lives. Again, the majority of victims do not go on to become adolescent or adult perpetrators; and those who do perpetrate in adolescence usually don't perpetrate as adults if they get help when they are young.

Myth #7—If the perpetrator is female, the boy or adolescent should consider himself fortunate to have been initiated into heterosexual activity.

In reality, premature or coerced sex, whether by a mother, aunt, older sister, babysitter, or other female in a position of power over a boy, causes confusion at best, and rage, depression, or other problems in more negative circumstances. To be used as a sexual object by a more powerful person, male or female, is always abusive and often damaging.

Believing these myths is dangerous and damaging.

- So long as society believes these myths, and teaches them to children from their earliest years, sexually abused males will be unlikely to get the recognition and help they need.

- So long as society believes these myths, sexually abused males will be more likely to join the minority of survivors who perpetuate this suffering by abusing others.

- So long as boys or men who have been sexually abused believe these myths, they will feel ashamed and angry.

- And so long as sexually abused males believe these myths, they reinforce the power of another devastating myth that all abused children struggle with: that it was their fault. It is never the fault of the child in a sexual situation—though perpetrators can be quite skilled at getting their victims to believe these myths and take on the responsibility that is always and only their own.

For any male who has been sexually abused, becoming free of these myths is an essential part of the recovery process.

The shame of the event, the repeated rejection by his father, the questioning of his own gender, the anger that results from such abuse, and the humiliation of having to go home and report this to his mother—all that was above and beyond what any child should have to suffer.

By the time Rick was in his late teens, he was gone from home. There seemed to be nothing or no one there for his comfort and support. Wounded repeatedly, self-worth in the garbage can, he attempted to make some kind of a life for himself. How does a kid survive all of this alone? There has to be some way of coping with the feelings of belonging nowhere. If his parents didn't care and didn't want him, who would?

In an article by Dennis A. Balcom, these statements are found:

> *Many adult **sons** abandoned by their **fathers** have difficulty developing and sustaining self-esteem, forming lasting emotional attachments, recognizing their feelings, or being expressive with their adult partners and children. These men must turn their attention toward their absent **fathers** and resolve the mystery of their absence to ensure that their current intimate relationships can succeed.*

The Journal of Men's Studies. March 22, 1998.

If and until any help is sought by an abandoned son, how does he cope? One coping method often used is an addiction to a substance, an activity, or a mode of thinking. Usually the rejected are absolutely addicted to the thought that they do not belong, are unworthy of love and acceptance, and will never truly be accepted by anyone. At the same time, these victims have no idea how to connect to other individuals, especially on an intimate level, and especially those within their adult family unit.

An article written by a well-experienced psychologist, Dr. Jim Hopper, contains some excellent material about male-to-male abuse in childhood. Dr. Hopper is a clinical psychologist and researcher who has studied the lasting effects of child abuse, including the long-term effects of childhood sexual abuse in men. He is also a clinical instructor of psychology in the Department of Psychiatry at the Harvard Medical School. In this article, we read:

Factors research has shown to influence the effects of abuse:

- Age of the child when the abuse happened. Younger is usually more damaging, but different effects are associated with different developmental periods.

- Who committed the abuse. Effects are generally worse when it was a parent, stepparent or trusted adult than a stranger.

- Whether the child told anyone, and if so, the person's response. Doubting, ignoring, blaming and shaming responses can be extremely damaging—in some cases even more than the abuse itself.

- Whether or not violence was involved, and if so, how severe.

- How long the abuse went on.

Additional factors that are difficult to research or may differ in significance for different people:

- Whether the abuse involved deliberately humiliating the child.

- How "normal" such abuse was in the extended family and local culture.

- Whether the child had loving family members, and/or knew that *someone* loved her or him.

- Whether the child had some good relationships—with siblings, friends, teachers, coaches, etc.

- Whether the child had relationships in which "negative" feelings were acceptable, and could be expressed and managed safely and constructively.

Some of these factors are about how <u>severe</u> the abuse was, and some are about the <u>relational context</u> of the abuse and the child's reactions. Both types of factors are extremely important.

A great deal of research has been conducted, and continues to be conducted, on how such factors determine outcomes for those abused in childhood. Factors that increase the likelihood of negative outcomes have been referred to as "risk factors," and ones that decrease the likelihood of negative outcomes as "protective factors." Every person who has experienced abuse is unique. And every person who has experienced abuse has a unique combination of risk and protective factors that have influenced, and continue to influence, the effects in his or her life.

In summary, it is important to appreciate that these issues are very complex, and to be familiar with how abuse and neglect can—*depending on a variety of other factors*—affect various aspects of a person's life. Keep this in mind as you search the web for information and understanding about the effects of child abuse.

Potential Long-Term Effects of the Sexual Abuse of Males

This section lists *potential*, but not inevitable, lasting effects of the sexual abuse of male children. It should not be read as a "laundry list" of problems and symptoms that necessarily follow the sexual abuse of males, nor does the presence of any in males with sexual abuse histories necessarily mean the abuse is their primary cause. (See above.)

Findings on the long-term effects of child sexual abuse in males have been more consistent than those on prevalence. Methodologies for detecting problems and symptoms that could be outcomes are relatively straightforward, and many studies have utilized standardized measures that are widely accepted in the field.

First, I want to recommend a paper by David Lisak, Ph.D. This paper contains many powerful quotations from interviews with male survivors of sexual abuse. Lisak groups the quotations into themes, and discusses them with remarkable insight and compassion. The themes are:

- Anger
- Fear
- Homosexuality Issues
- Helplessness
- Isolation and Alienation
- Legitimacy
- Loss
- Masculinity Issues
- Negative Childhood Peer Relations
- Negative Schemas about People
- Negative Schemas about the Self
- Problems with Sexuality
- Self-Blame/Guilt
- Shame/Humiliation

Like Ron and Sam, Rick was actually brilliant. He trained and excelled at his chosen career until an unfortunate accident caused him a severe injury after which, out of necessity, that career ended.

Rick found a girl who sincerely loved him and with whom he felt connected and accepted. They dated for a while, during which time his addiction did not surface. Once they were married for a couple of years, however, the atmosphere in their home began to change. Rick and his wife Misty discovered that they were about to have a baby. Things seemed to go well during the pregnancy, but as the time for delivery drew near, Rick became more and more uneasy. His uneasiness was at first undetected, but when Misty went into labor, Rick began to panic. After their son was born, he went out and got drunk. The more attention Misty paid to their baby, the more aggravated Rick became.

Alcohol consumption became a common occurrence. Dissatisfaction with his job escalated his frustration, which caused him to drink more. When he drank, he became verbally abusive to Misty, and his baby suffered the consequences of the tense atmosphere at home. For him, Misty could do nothing right. In actuality, Rick was dumping onto her the angst he felt toward his mother, who, without having abandoned him physically, certainly had done so on an emotional level. The odd thing is that Rick's wife was very much unlike his mother, especially with regard to their children, so what he was experiencing in his home and relationships was abnormal to him.

Two more children were born to Rick and Misty. A business had been started, and Misty's father was involved in it. Because he was emotionally healthy compared to Rick's own father, Rick could not stand being in his presence, so he left the business and found another job. Rick hated that job, too, and as his frustration with his career escalated, so did his drinking and his verbal abuse toward his wife and his children. Somehow, son number one seemed to get the greater portion of his anger, but

Misty took the worst of it. Rick would drink himself nearly into oblivion, and then his rage would erupt; he would rant for hours against Misty.

The frustration was above and beyond for Misty, who, by that point, was coping with a full-time business, three children, and an alcoholic and abusive husband. Being constantly demeaned lowered her self-worth, until finally she decided she needed to find someone who would adore her. As an attractive and friendly woman, that was no difficult task. A short affair on her part led Rick to retaliate with an affair of his own.

Urged, of course, by Misty, Rick went to four rehabilitation sessions. Each time he would return sober, but that would last for only a few weeks. Finally Rick sought help from a co-worker who recommended a counselor whom he thought could help. For several months he saw the counselor sporadically, and did get some help; but the bouts of heavy drinking, and rants against Misty, continued. It seemed that whatever she did or didn't do, said or didn't say, or expressed facially would irritate him and be interpreted as though she were rejecting him.

We usually say that *"rejected people look for rejection under every rock, and if they can't find it, they will manufacture it."* This statement is truer than most would believe.

Rick continued to self-sabotage his family life, his career, and his marriage. No matter how embarrassed he was after an event of ranting against his wife and children, no matter how physically ill he became as a result of the stress, the drinking, and the unresolved emotional issues, he just couldn't seem to commit himself to a rehabilitation program or counseling.

Mark R. Leary is a professor of psychology at Wake Forest University and author of the book *Interpersonal Rejection*. In his book he states, on page 8:

People who are highly rejection sensitive, for example, inter-pret even minor slights and insensitive behavior as evidence that others do not value. Similarly, people who have low trait self-esteem, who are socially anxious, depressed or narcissistic, or who have an insecure attachment style often see more rejection in people's rejection than is warranted.

Actually, one friend who was severely rejected in childhood used to say to me (Nancy), "Why would you want anything to do with me. I'm a mess! You'll give up this friendship some-time along the way. There's no way it'll last." Certainly, I did not feel this way toward her. Actually, I loved her dearly, and we had enjoyed lots of fun together. As far as I was concerned, this friendship would last forever! Persistence has paid off!

Ron tells of his friend who was severely rejected in childhood and who suspected everyone of doing him wrong. Of course, Ron never dreamed that his friend would accuse him; but, sure enough, an accusation was made, along with threats, and that relationship has ended. How does Ron feel about that? Devas-tated! Ron prays for this man frequently in hopes that someday he will recant and be willing to re-establish the friendship.

This is the hard part about rejection—it is a lifelong feeling that can only be reduced by consistent work on the part of the victim, work that will take him or her back to the original cause of these feelings of rejection. It is through this in-depth work of investigating, coming to understand, and forgiving (letting go of the need to repay that individual for rejecting you) that healing can take place.

Rick just couldn't seem to stop his drinking. Even though his relationship with his counselor was an excellent, trusting one, the merry-go-round on which he found himself was spinning faster and faster. In an attempt to cope with and understand the depth of her husband's pain, Misty began participating in a small group for recovery from childhood wounds. Of course, we as humans tend to marry our emotional equals; and even though Misty's childhood had not been as harsh as Rick's, she still had a few issues of her own. We are attracted to our emotional equals, although sometimes courtship's strange parade can mask some of what is really inside a person. Misty's choice to look at herself was an encouragement to Rick, and it even helped him to make the choice to seek additional help from a special physician that his counselor had recommended. Still, however, Rick attended counseling sessions very sporadically, and he did not follow the guidelines of the physicians, counselors, and other experts who were trying to help him. But his small group was a constant support and blessing to him when he attended, because it helped him to realize that he was not the only one who suffered the pain of rejection.

Unfortunately, Rick became a God-hater. He isn't sure that God exists; and, as far as Rick is concerned, if God does exist, he isn't worth honoring. Rick feels that God forsook him when he needed God the most. Would offering religion in this instance be of help? Not at all! He would only rebel further!

Are we saying here that a relationship with God would not have been of value to Rick? Not at all! What we are saying is that Rick needs to identify his wounds and acknowledge the results of his pain in his adult life. He needs to apply valuable information to himself, and that is why we are including it in this book. Rick needs to work through his wounds by verbally sharing and writing out letters to those who wounded him. These letters are not for retribution or revenge against his perpetrators, but rather to acknowledge his wounds and their results in his life. Writing is an action component which has been proven to make a dramatic difference to those who will do the work.

Once the writing is complete, Rick needs to take it to his counselor and read aloud what his hand has written. In so doing, his eyes see what he has written, his mouth speaks the words, and his ears hear them. This gives his mind and heart the message that the issue is being cared for, and then forgiveness can come.

As Rick would soften by emptying his anger and resentment, his heart would open to allow God (as he terms it, "one of my perpetrators") to provide forgiveness in his heart and mind so that he can offer it to those who wounded him.

What has become of Rick? Have all the attempts at repairing his fragile self and returning him to an experience of normalcy been beneficial? Stay tuned!

Chapter Four

Women Feel Rejection Too!

While it is true that men are more negatively impacted by rejection, especially if they are rejected by their mothers, it is also true that women know and feel the negative effects of rejection as well.

I've told this story before many times. As I write it now, I still recall the heart-wrenching scenes of my father deriding me for whatever reason he wanted to that day. Yes, I see the scenes, I experience the sadness; but I no longer feel that it's necessary to make my husband pay the price for what my father did or did not do.

Women usually marry men who remind them in some way of their fathers. I know now that I did; but back when we were dating, and even when we got engaged, I did not see it. I didn't see the anger just beneath the surface of his everyday behaviors. He was sweet and kind and very thoughtful of me. Every Friday he would give me a long-stemmed red rose. Every weekend we managed to see each other, one way or another, even though we lived about a hundred miles apart. When I worked at the hospital over the weekend, he came to me; and when I was off for the weekend, I took the train to his town. Always there was the rose, a passionate kiss, and a tender and loving time together.

The bubble burst, however, the first day of our honeymoon. We had taken a ferry across the sound to a remote island, where we would be spending the week. As we were getting off the ferry, Ron twisted his ankle, and down he went. As I look back on it, I am sure he was embarrassed to have fallen on the first day of his honeymoon. But when I put my arms around him and asked what I could do to help, reassuring him of my love, he threw his arms wide open and hollered, "Leave me alone!" I had to jump out of the way of his arms or else I would have fallen into the water. As soon as the excruciating pain left him, he was fine. No apologies, but his mood certainly switched!

Because I knew his background, and because I loved him dearly and was so grateful to God for the man he had given me, I was very affectionate—let's say I was all over him—that honeymoon week. On day five, he pushed me away and shouted, "Leave me alone! What did I do, marry a slut?"

I was devastated! A slut I was not! During our ten months of dating there had been no sex; but now, having been through a ceremony and carrying a marriage certificate, I thought that we had gained the privilege of sexual intimacy.

What I did not realize at the time was that Ron had never known affection or sexual intimacy without a price. Here he was, getting all he ever wanted with personal love and affection, but it felt like abuse to him. *Whatever is unknown and not experienced does feel like abuse.*

Responding to his demand, I pulled away, disheartened and sad. How could this wonderful, loving man turn so nasty, so different? I guessed I really was the worthless woman that I had felt I was all of my life. His behavior toward me had to be my fault, I thought.

For years following the honeymoon I still felt worthless. Somehow, I felt like I had failed the man I adored; I had disappointed him. So our intimacy, rather than coming from a place of pure love and adoration, was based on my emptiness and worthlessness, and on his as well. I was giving him all I had, but it could not fill the vacant space where his maternal love should have been. I knew that I wasn't enough, but I had already felt that throughout my childhood from the other man in my life.

I was born shortly before my father was sent overseas as a medic specialist during the second World War. I spent my first four years living with my mother and her parents, a warm and loving English couple. I was the center of their world, and I knew and felt their abundant love for me. Grandma was warm and cuddly, and so was my mother, for most of that time. Her velvety nurse hands held and caressed me often, and I felt cherished by those three adults in my life.

My mother had become pregnant right before Dad was sent overseas, and months later my baby brother appeared. Due to an accident in the hospital, his life was only ten days long. My mother and her parents went into mourning, and that lasted a long time. In addition, there was the war that had taken my mother's loving and supportive husband away, and she pined for him as well. The house was filled with sadness, and I now realize that the grey cloud that floated above and around me for years was formed at a very young age. Would some Army officer arrive at the house to give us devastating news of my father's death on the battlefield? How would my father react when he found out that his son had died needlessly? What would life be like when he finally did come home?

It was during this time of mourning that I first felt the pain of rejection. My poor mother was so consumed by the grief from the loss of her son that she didn't have much time for a two-and-a-half-year-old. My grandparents had to work during the day, and my mother worked some 3:00–11:00 p.m. shifts at the hospital where baby Jimmy had died. Each shift she worked was a bold reminder of her loss.

When the war was over and my father came home, he was an absolute stranger to me and spent much of his time alone with my mother. Almost immediately after he came home, he found an apartment for mother and me, and I was taken away from my loving and cuddly grandma and grandpa. I was devastated, and I did whatever I could to stay at their home nearly every weekend.

As I look back on it, I am sure that my father loved me in his own way—as best he could. Sadly, I could never seem to "do it right" for him! Many years later, as a mature adult, my husband and I took a trip to England to find relatives of my father. We were blessed to find Eric, my father's first cousin and a retired commander in the British Navy. He and I went for a walk with his dog, and I asked what he knew about my father's parents. When he told me that my grandmother's name was not allowed to be mentioned in his home, I was surprised and confused, even though I did remember her as being a bit of a spitfire. Then he stopped me, put his hands gently on my face, and told me that my grandmother was an "evil woman." I thought that was rather dramatic coming from a proper British gentleman, but nonetheless he had said it, and I believed him.

The stories of my father's mother told that she was a great cook, and frankly I do remember her pies and her fish and chips—they were out of this world! But I also remember her attitude, and it was always negative. Her words were often curt or nasty. Eric continued, "You know why your grandmother was the way she was, don't you?" he questioned. "I have no idea," I replied. "Well, her father was an alcoholic, a drunk, and when she was a girl and he was inebriated, he was cruel to her. The sad thing is this: When your grandmother's father was a boy, his father was a tin miner in the south of England. The tin mines closed, so, in order to support his family, he boarded a boat for South America to mine tin there. The boat was lost at sea, and, of course, he was never heard from again. His mother had to go to the mill to work, and he was left to manage alone while she worked long hours during the day and spent her evenings mourning her loss rather than paying attention to her child."

WOW! I was the third generation from him, and I had always felt the effects of my great-grandfather's abandonment and rejection through my father's behaviors. My grandmother had been very cruel to my father, absolutely rejecting him, while his father, a kind and gentle man, seemed to take a back seat to his powerful wife. She hated men because of how her father had treated her, and so she treated both men in her life, her husband and her son, with great disdain!

Actually, I remember that, when I was a teenager, my grandmother had a stroke that left her aphasic (unable to talk) and paralyzed on one side. She ended up in a nursing home for a total of nine years before her death. My father visited her almost every night after work, and, even in her state, she would shake her little finger and angrily shout "da-da-da-da-da" at him. My poor Dad never got a break from her angst, and yet he was kind and loving toward her. I am sure that as a child he hoped and dreamed for just a few kind words from her, but instead he often heard her talking against him to her friends. My grandfather, whom my Dad loved dearly, died of stomach cancer while my Dad was overseas during the war, around the time of the birth and death of my brother.

Somehow, I couldn't do anything right for my father. He was a brilliant scholar of the Bible, an accomplished pianist who had trained at the Juilliard School of Music in New York City, and also a fine cabinet maker. Some of the things he made still decorate our home. I remember hauling rocks with him every Sunday so that he could build stone walls. Finally, when I went to England, I understood what my father was doing by creating all those stone walls: He was building what he remembered of the fields, which were separated by curving stone walls, where he and Eric had roamed and played as children.

As a child, I couldn't play the piano in the manner he could. I was not the A+ scholar that he was, and as a result I caught his demeaning remarks frequently. I was scared of him. At a piano recital where I was to play (and where, of course, he sat in the front row) I got to the piano and froze. I couldn't remember a thing—not the notes, not the name of the piece I was to play, and certainly not how to start. He was mortified, and so was I. I just returned to my seat and cried quietly. His disgusted sigh could be heard throughout the auditorium. The promised ice cream cone didn't happen that night, and his silence in the car on the ride home was deafening. When we pulled into the driveway, his angry words blurted out, and I sunk into the corner, thumb in my mouth, and cried while he yelled.

I was an adult wife and mother when the worst incident occurred. We were sitting together—mother, father, Hubby, and me—having a dish of ice cream. Out of the blue, he spoke to me: "Poode (the nickname he had called me for years), you are a great disappointment to me," he blurted out. I was stunned! Again, my feelings of worthlessness were confirmed. But, as usual, I bit my lip and said, "*Really, Dad? Why is that?*"

He went on to tell me that I was fine when I was working as an RN, but since I had left nursing and returned to graduate school for a degree in marriage and family therapy, I was now quitting my work for God and moving on to working for His enemy. There was no refuting him, as my father felt that anything in the field of psychology was "of the devil." "*Sorry you feel this way, Dad,*" was all I could say in response.

Half an hour after we all went off to bed, we heard and felt a giant thud in the house. Ron sat upright and said, "*Your Dad!*" as he bounced out of bed and down the stairs to the kitchen, with me following right after him. Sure enough, there was my father on the floor. We did our best to bring him back to life using all the training and experience nursing had given me, but to no avail. My father died in my arms just the way Ron's father had died in his arms when he was a 16-year-old teen.

It took some time, and the knowledge that came from our visit to England, to understand my father and his behavior. It was only then that I came to realize that my father had treated me in the ways he had been treated by the generation above him. Once I understood his beginnings, I was able to "let him off the hook" for how I fared. But the truth is that, in actuality, I was the one off the hook, because *those who refuse to forgive are the ones carrying the burden!*

Had I not allowed forgiveness to flow from God through me toward my father, even though he was deceased, I would have carried the baggage forever, and my husband would have paid the price for my father's behaviors.

How had my father's rejection affected me? I expected poor Ron to fill the big holes that my relationship with my father had left in me. If Ron's behaviors seemed even remotely similar to my father's, he paid the price for what both he and my father had done. I expected Ron to be the affectionate, giving, generous, accepting man that my father was only to a degree—only when I performed correctly in his eyes. *That's the way a daughter's relationship with her father—or lack of relationship—impacts her future marriage. She will look for a man who will be to her what her father was or was not in her connection to him. If her father is absent physically and/or emotionally, she will have a desperate need to have her emptiness filled, and she will seek a man early on in her teen years and even be attracted to men of all ages while still a child.*

It has now been proven by science that every child needs a male parent and a female parent. The male parent is to be the provider, protector and priest. The female parent is to be the compassionate, concerned caregiver.

Dr. Evoy, in his book entitled *The Rejected,* has much to say about parental expectations:

> *The acceptance a number of individuals had received from their parents was conditional on their being able to fulfill certain specific, frustrated parental ambitions or desires. They were rewarded with warm acceptance in direct proportion to the success they achieved in fulfilling such parental longings. Almost without exception, those who were given the option chose with considerable resentment, to fulfill the dictated parental terms rather than to go without rewarding responses.*

Page 18.

In some instances parental terms were spelled out only in a general way. Their children came to feel that rewards were to be earned by constantly striving to fulfill the entire range of expectations the parents held for them.

Page 19.

Others learned from their parents that they had to earn all acceptance and affection.

Page 19.

How well I understand these statements. I knew that it was expected of me, at all times, to be the good girl and the example of goodness and proper deportment to all other children. It was a standard far too high for me to accomplish, yet I worked at it untiringly. I felt that if I failed, I would be unloved, and that thought was intolerable. My parents chose my clothes, and they were entirely different from what my peers were wearing. Wearing them got me rejected and scorned by my peers. It was only once, when I was sixteen, that I lied to my parents in a way, telling them that I was going to a masquerade party with a male friend from school when the party was really a dance. My father was absolutely determined that no daughter of his would dance. I did have a great time and thoroughly enjoyed my date, but twinges of guilt kept haunting me all evening because I had rebelled.

My story is one of outright rejection, seeable and easily understandable, at least by me. Other people who knew my father, and the picture he portrayed outside the home, boldly disagree.

Others have endured rejection that seems hidden or less obnoxious because it didn't come from outright statements such as "You don't belong!" It may have been initiated in the womb by a mother who was afraid of her pregnancy or who did not have a good relationship with her baby's birth father. It may have been that the mother's health was compromised while the child was in the womb. A difficult delivery can cause negative feelings and hyperanxiety. As for unlawful or criminal acts, I dared not! But the anger and resentment that I held inside ended up hurting me and my daughters.

MARIA'S STORY

Children who are conceived and/or born out of wedlock also experience feelings of rejection. Maria was conceived between her mother and a boyfriend. When Maria was born, her birth father came by to see his girlfriend two or three times in two years. At first, Maria's mother lived with her mother; and, in order to provide for her mother and her daughter, Maria's mother left her mother's home and moved to the city for a job when Maria was two years old. Maria was left with her grandmother.

Was Maria purposely rejected by her father? Probably not, but she seldom saw him again. Was Maria rejected by her mother when she went to the city to work? Well, the truth is that she was abandoned by her mother, not purposefully rejected, and not purposefully abandoned. Maria's mother simply needed to provide food, clothing and shelter for her mother and her child. But does the child know the difference?

Can a small child reason from cause to effect? The answer is no. That kind of reasoning doesn't develop in a child until puberty when the left frontal part of the brain is developing. All the child knows is that her mother has left her, and she reasons that it must be her fault. Not having a father like other kids do, his showing up for a half-hour visit when she was less than two years of age is far less than what the child needs. What it does create is immense insecurity in the child because the father should be the provider, protector and priest. As a result, in adulthood, possessing things seems to offer a small sense of security, and for some becomes an addiction.

So today, as a grown woman, Maria clings to her mother tenaciously. Her mother is the only reality she has that connects her to her beginnings and assures her that she does truly exist. Providing for her mother and giving her everything she wants is a compulsion within Maria. It's almost as if she is saying, *"I have to do whatever it takes to assure myself that she will not leave me again."*

In Mark R. Leary's book *Interpersonal Rejection*, he states:

> *Although this is sometimes true, sad withdrawal and lethargy often prolong the dysphoric (negative) state and impede the formation of new relationships and for that matter, engagement in alternative relationships that already exist. Furthermore other people soon grow tired of those who are chronically unhappy, both because dysphoric (negative) moods are contagious and because unhappy people tend to make excessive demands on others' time and patience. Evidence suggests that depressed people cause other people to distance themselves so that they aren't required to excessively provide reassurance and consolation.*

Page 151.

Unfortunately, rejected people, especially those who have been rejected early on in childhood by their parents, tend to constantly look for someone who will fill the giant hole left in them. They long for someone to take on the responsibility of a parent to them. This annoys others who have lives of their own. They think, feel, or even know that their own parents have rejected them.

Is there any way into the hearts and minds of these rejected ones? Many have been hardened by life experiences. Perhaps they have committed crimes that have resulted in incarceration. So many are simply wounded individuals who lash out at those whom they feel have rejected them. One wise woman said that the reason why there are so many hard-hearted men and women in this world is that the better part of their nature was dwarfed and perverted in childhood, and, unless the rays of divine light can melt their hard-heartedness, the lives of those around them will be forever miserable.

There is a way to heal the wounds of rejection, at least to the point where every moment of every day is not orchestrated by old rejection. If we would benefit those who hurt because of rejection, we will do what it takes to teach and reassure them so that they can experience acceptance at its best.

Chapter Five

Why Only Some?

Perhaps by now you are asking yourself, "Why is it that some people are able to make something positive out of their lives, and others suffer and cause others to suffer also? What makes the difference? The answer to that question has several ingredients. In this chapter we will look at the wounded one as an individual, with the abilities, thoughts, feelings, and detriments of the one, considering that so many factors play into who a person is and what he or she becomes.

We have already learned that a child's earliest experiences, beginning in the womb, greatly influence the developing child. Relationships are very important! Now we are going to look at the inborn differences that are God-given, experience-influenced, and tweaked as development occurs.

No two people are exactly alike. While two people may be very similar in some areas, they cannot and will not be identical. WHY? The answer has multiple reasons. First, they didn't have the same parents. They were not born under the same circumstances, thinking styles, and in-womb experiences. They did not have the same newborn, infant, or early childhood environment or experiences. And they were not given the same gift when they were conceived. In this chapter we will look at the four types of brain gifts based on the physiology of the brain. We will examine the four quadrants, or chunks, of brain tissue and the characteristics, abilities, and thinking styles of each.

For years we studied and taught the four temperament types as identified by Hippocrates many years ago. We took the test created and offered by Robert J. Cruise and W. Peter Blitchington and taught extensively by Tim and Beverly LaHaye. We identified our own temperaments. We took training to be able to test others and have taught countless seminars on the subject. It always seemed to us that something was missing, but we weren't sure just what. And then we took another inventory.

This one identified the quadrant of our brains that is most highly oxygenated; that is, because of its higher oxygen content, the one that works with greater ease or less resistance, making life easier, less stressful, less complicated, and healthier. We took the training to better understand it, and then we went to the originators of the concept and took more training. Still something was missing.

What we *finally* felt had been missing from each of these inventories was the taking into account of the in-womb and early childhood experiences of those being tested. We could definitely identify current behaviors; the temperament inventory did that very well. We could look at what the other inventory identified as brain gifts. But how much did early experience impact the results of those inventories? So we created an inventory using input from the originator of the Brain Lead Inventory, *Hermann International*, and with their blessing added the component of early experience. What we have discovered has verified what the ACE Study stated: that early experience impacts most areas of our lives today, including physical well-being.

THE HUMAN BRAIN

The brain of a human is divided into four (4) major chunks of brain tissue, each with layers and components. Each of these chunks of tissue has specific attributes, and in healthy individuals they all work together to facilitate all of the functions of the brain.

Every individual is born with one, and occasionally two or three, of these components gifted with more oxygen than the others. This quadrant or chunk has the ability to function with greater ease because of its higher level of oxygen concentration.

Each of these quadrants has specific qualities, both positive and negative. These qualities contribute to and are part of the foundation of who each person becomes, along with in-womb and life experiences. Taking a look at these brain quadrants will assist you in identifying which of yours is gifted with the higher level of oxygen and therefore works with greater ease and contains the attributes that you identify as yours.

Brain divided into four quadrants.

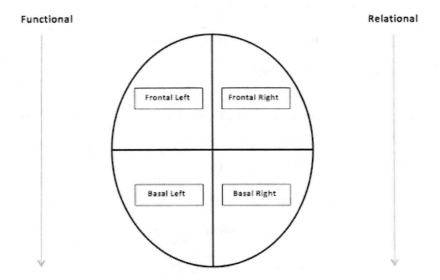

The vertical line down the center of the brain is known as the **corpus calossum.** It is a very thick band of neurons that connect the two (right and left) hemispheres of the brain so that the **relational side** (the two right quadrants) can work in tandem with the **functional side** (the two left quadrants).

There are a few frontal to basal and basal to frontal connectors, known as **laterals. But . . . there are NO connectors that are kitty-corner!!**

Living life without accessing the quadrant of your brain that is most gifted can cause many emotional and health-related issues.

The right hemisphere is known as the relational brain. It is:

- **Visual**—Sees everything in picture form

- **Subjective**—Perceives its own reality (may be different from actual)

- **Impulsive**—Instinctive and spontaneous

- **Imaginative**—Has lively imagination

- **Intuitive**—Looks beyond the obvious

The left hemisphere is more logical in its capacity and function. It is:

- **Functional**—Makes things work

- **Objective**—Deals with facts

- **Analytical**—Skilled in reasoning

- **Deductive**—Draws conclusions by reasoning

- **Realistic**—Factual

The Four Brain Quadrants

Each of the hemispheres of the brain has two main areas—the **frontal** and the **basal**. That means that there are four main areas of the brain. These areas have specific abilities and specialties, and they are highly specialized chunks: basal (or back) left and basal right, frontal left and frontal right. Each of the four lobes has its own specialized screens or filters that cause it to perceive only what is necessary to do its job.

Each and every day, we use all four quadrants of our brains. Everyone needs and uses the abilities found in each of the quadrants, but usually one quadrant stands out from the four as a personal specialty. Some individuals have two that are highly gifted, and a very few are proficient in three of the quadrants. However, in every individual, one quadrant is most highly gifted.

The frontal left perceives function and functional relationships. It excels in what supports what, with what degree of tolerance, and what blocks what. In other words, it *knows* the big picture of what components relate and work together. People gifted in this quadrant want to know about each component of a machine, plan, etc. and how it works with the others to perform a function. They are gifted in logical analysis and can calculate, evaluate, diagnose and prescribe effectively. In addition, the frontal left chunk excels at directing, prioritizing and strategizing.

The basal left sees bounded shapes or masses that it labels with words it hears and uses. It prefers to grasp and handle in order to produce a product (hands-on work), is specialized in sequencing, and excels at performing routine tasks. It breaks things down bit by bit, step by step. It can appear to be objectively detached, and it can gain control by use of rules, orders, structures and systems. It processes information and creates things such as divisions of labor or class, chains of command, color coding, etc.

The basal right perceives the presence or absence of harmonic relationships (aural, visual, physical, or kinesthetic—sensation of movement) in its environment and acts to establish harmony and connection where they are missing. It excels at building good will, trust and loyalty, and it is the basis for peace, cooperation and collaboration. It is very sensitive to facial expressions, tones of voice, and body language so that the person can create harmonious relationships.

The frontal right perceives abstract patterns and relationships and sees pictures in place of words. It can perceive the abstraction or caricature of a face. It is gifted at seeing trends; these signal change and trigger the imagination to invent a successful response to the change noticed (product, service, strategy). It is superbly suited to help us adapt to change. Children who are gifted in this quadrant are often diagnosed as having ADD or ADHD. They have difficulty sitting still because their body desires and needs to move as rapidly as the ideas and pictures bombarding their minds.

We believe that babies are born as right-brainers out of their need to connect and harmonize with parents and significant others. If a child lives in a chaotic or abusive environment, we believe that the basal right child, in whom harmony is of utmost importance, will do whatever is necessary to attempt to maintain peace. The child will be a conformist and a people-pleaser, and his or her behaviors will be designed to "not rock the boat." If things get too rough in the environment and these children need to escape, they have easy access to the basal left quadrant, where they can hide. As they get older, they learn that there are certain things that they can control: their toys, any of their possessions, their clothes, and their "blankies." These things give them comfort and a sense that, at least in their own little worlds, they can be in control.

The frontal right child is a creative visionary who can think up "innovative" ways to deal with their hurtful environment or family members. The frontal right has easy access to the frontal left quadrant, where not only is analysis located but also anger is found. These children would more than likely be the aggressive ones; they do not so much have a fear of hurting others but rather will jump right into their novel ideas to get their needs met: "If I can't get what I need from my family (love, tenderness, food, attention), I will TAKE whatever I want that will make me feel better." So these children, even at a young age, become little thieves who take shiny, pretty things to make them feel better about who they are.

Often these children learn to adapt to a quadrant of their brain that is not their God-given one, and because of this, after living in their ungifted quadrant for some time, develop symptoms that are physically and emotionally unhealthy.

Living outside of your original gift can and usually will result in the devastating condition known as PASS—Prolonged Adaption Stress Syndrome.

Commonly observed symptoms of PASS include the following, which may be present in varying degrees in individuals who have been falsifying type or adapting (chronically living outside of their giftedness). They are:

1. **FATIGUE**—A growing fatigue not alleviated by sleep

- Increased need for sleep but interference with the quality of sleep

- Decreased dreaming

- Exhaustion

- Tendency to crave specific foods or high fat/sugar snacks for "quick energy," producing weight gain with its stressors

- Tendency to self-medicate, attempting to alter brain chemistry (the neurotransmitter ratios); often accomplished by alcohol, nicotine, or caffeine ingestion

2. **HYPERVIGILANCE**—Protective alertness for safety

- The brain can be temporarily pushed to introversion, requiring increased energy to maintain this level of alertness (to keep the lens of the brain open wider)

- Increased sensitivity to environmental stimuli (light, sound, odors); this can impact relationships

- Change in activities; previously enjoyed activities can be discarded in favor of less gregarious ones; a person may appear to be isolating but is doing so to decrease stimulation

3. **IMMUNE SYSTEM ALTERATION**—Individual "living a lie" or falsifying type

- Falsifying type can suppress immune system function (temporarily shrinks the thymus gland), which can negatively impact one's health

- Slower rate of healing after cut or abrasion

- Increased autoimmune disease symptoms

- Increased susceptibility to illness

- Increased risk of developing cancer

4. **MEMORY IMPAIRMENT**—Cortisol, released under stress, can interfere with memory functions

- Decreased ability to lay down a memory, store data in long-term memory, or access/recall memory at a later date

- Diminished neurotransmitter function reduces effective neuron communication; the *"phone lines are down"*; the mind becomes *"muddled"* with a reduced ability to concentrate

5. **ALTERED BRAIN CHEMISTRY**—prolonged adaption can interfere with the hypothalamus and pituitary function, upsetting hormonal balance

- Decreased growth hormone

- Decreased insulin secretion

- Decreased reproductive functions

- Increased production of glucocorticoids, prematurely aging the hippocampus (which is used to lay down memories in time and space)

- Possible alteration in permeability of the blood brain barrier

6. **DIMINISHED FRONTAL LOBE FUNCTIONS**—the frontal lobe is concerned with moral judgment, will, decision making and spirituality

- Decrease in artistic/creative endeavors (e.g. writer's block)

- Reduced ability to brainstorm options

- Reduced ability to choose "best" option in critical situation

- Interference with logical/rational decision making

- Increased injuries due to distraction and/or making mistakes

- Slowed speed and decreased clarity of thinking

7. **DISCOURAGEMENT AND/OR DEPRESSION**

- Repeated triggering of conserve/withdraw response to stress (especially true for high introverts)

- Can be seen in extroverts who perceive a mismatch between who they are and society's expectations or repeated failures

- 20 million U.S. citizens are depressed, and 15% are suicidal; PASS is a contributing factor in some

8. **SELF-WORTH PROBLEMS**

- Individual can take on "victim" role or endeavor to be all things to all people

- The pendulum—individual swings from one extreme to another—sometimes seen in professional invalidation, but validated personally with a small group of friends; the dichotomy can be confusing, unnerving and disconcerting as the individual tries unsuccessfully to be seen as successful in both areas

  This material was prepared by Arlene Taylor, Ph.D. and Katherine Benziger, Ph.D. and synthesized by Ron Rockey, Ph.D. and Nancy A. Rockey, Ph.D.

This is a lot of information to absorb, isn't it? Just when you thought you had pinpointed which quadrant(s) of the brain contained your gift, you learned about falsification. That's a major "aha" for lots of people!

You see, we are often forced into falsifying in childhood and adolescence in an attempt to make Mom and Dad happy. We kick against what we know is true for us hoping that we will get the attention that we need, but often it is impossible to please those who are most important to us!

Chapter Six

Darker Than It Seems!

Hollywood thinks it has it all—that there, in the movie capital of the world, live the greatest performers of all time. But, in reality, many common, ordinary people are really the greatest performers of all! Many of us learned very early in life how we should behave and how to perform so that we will be accepted, and, for sure, everyone wants to be accepted!

The opposite of rejection is acceptance. Being accepting, which includes listening, understanding, showing compassion, and caring, is the only way to even get near someone who has suffered severe rejection. And even then they may ask, "What do you want? No one has ever been kind to me without some kind of a hook. What's the hook?" Others may angrily push you away because, to them, nearness spells abuse.

Some will adamantly proclaim that they have not been rejected. They wear an image of "I've got it all together." These may work difficult or high-paying jobs because they have prepared themselves academically and experientially to hold positions of honor in order to experience acceptance. Such was the experience of Mike.

In a seminar we taught sat Mike and his wife Alana. Actually, they stood out from the rest of the crowd because they were attractive and very well dressed, and they presented a polished appearance. The seminar was at a church, and we came to find out that he was one of the leaders of the church, and so was his wife. They were punctual in returning to the auditorium as each session began, and we saw them attentively taking notes.

When the seminar was over, the pastor invited us to go out to a restaurant, and he had also invited several of the church leaders. Unknown to us, this was to be a meeting to discuss the details of starting the small group recovery program that we had offered. As the meal and the conversation progressed, Mike spoke up to comment that he was "one of the lucky ones": "I grew up in a good Christian home," he said, "and I have never suffered the abuse that you were teaching about. I was the second of two children, and my sister was older than me."

Mike went on to describe his home life with two professional parents, neither of whom was abusive in any way. His wife agreed with him that she too had been raised in a Christian home with no issues or problems at all.

You know, the statistics for homes and families where there are no difficulties or issues, and where childhood was sweet, loving and wholesome, are few and far between. As time passed in our acquaintance with this couple, we actually built a friendship and began to notice a pattern. Mike was addicted to work. He managed a large corporation, worked very long hours, and was very diligent and dedicated to his work and to pleasing his boss. However, not only did he have a full-time job plus, but he was also a wonderful cook. He frequently hosted dinner parties at his home, preparing luscious food that was perfectly presented. He was an officer in the church and was dedicated to seeing church growth and improvement.

Alana was also a hard worker. She kept her home so perfectly that *Better Homes and Gardens* could have knocked on the door at any hour of any day and filmed their perfectly appointed home in every room. She was extremely neat and organized, with a place for everything and everything in its place! She also worked part-time for her husband's boss designing and decorating his facilities, and they were elegantly done.

Some time passed, and Mike and Alana decided to attend the Binding the Wounds recovery classes at their church, not that they felt they had anything from which to recover. Before long, however, it began to dawn on Mike that his workaholism was the result of endeavoring to match up to his sister and finally gain the type of approval and acceptance from his parents that she seemed to have.

Children who are not treated equally in a family, or who feel that they were not treated the same, experience rejection too. Of course, it looks nothing like the rejection that Sam or Rick or Ron experienced, but it certainly was rejection. It caused Mike to spend years of his life trying to be good enough. It was quite an awakening for him to realize that he had perceived rejection because of comparison with his sibling—and, to be sure, if we perceive it, we receive it!

Children who are emotionally abused are also victims of rejection. Using words that are demeaning or names that are hurtful, ignoring children or telling them to be quiet—you know, "seen but not heard"—all these behaviors create within the victim the feeling that there is something wrong with them. They feel that they are not welcomed in the family and not considered valuable and important.

When I was seven or eight, I (Nancy) can remember my father hurling me off the piano bench, slapping my hands away from the keyboard, and calling me a "Big boob," all because I couldn't play the piano as well as he could. How could a young child who was fearful of her father play with the expression and expertise of a Juilliard man?

Victims of childhood sexual abuse, especially from a family member, also know what rejection feels like!

In a wonderful book entitled *The Wounded Heart,* author Dan Allender, Ph.D. writes about the typical reaction of Christians to abuse or words spoken about this subject:

> *There is a natural reluctance to face the problem. Christians seem to despise reality. We tend to be squeamish when look- ing at the destructive effects of sin. It is unpleasant to face the consequences of sin—our own and others'. To do so seems to discount the finished and sufficient work of our*

Savior. And so we pretend we're fine, when, in fact, we know that something is troubling our soul. A dull ache occasionally floats to the surface, or stalking memories return in dreams or in off thoughts during the day. But why bother about such strange feelings when our salvation is guaranteed and life's task is clear: trust and obey?

Page 12.

And so we shy away from helping the wounded whom we see on the streets, in the next pew, or at our workplace. We unaffectedly walk on by while the hurting are crying out for help. We tend to have no clue about the ravages of abuse, and we want to avoid the subject of sexual abuse at all costs.

However, Jesus Christ came to this earth to guarantee us a life here and now, not just the hope of a home in heaven where sin no longer reigns. Wouldn't it be great to take advantage of that life He offers us now?

In the case of sexual abuse, all too often the child is rejected as a child and put in the position of an adult just to satisfy the perverted sexual desires of another. One young girl—we'll call her Tammy—was the victim of her father's lust and actually bore his child. She told us how, after delivery, her father killed and buried the baby. What absolute desperation! How does a child or teen cope with this demoralizing experience? Would she feel loved and adored, or would she feel used?

Here's her take on it, not long after the incident, as a homeless and desperately hurting young woman:

Lord, I need a Friend

I'm calling from South Broadway, Lord
With no reason to pretend
You see, I'm with the homeless,
And Lord, I need a friend
The world just doesn't know
What it's like out on the street.
To always be looked down on,
And trampled by their feet.
There are times I am dirty
And my clothes look old and bad.
I know I don't smell good,
And my face looks drawn and sad.
So many just don't realize
That I'm lonely, and I'm cold
They forget I have a heart,
And they overlook my soul.
I want to stop this drinking, Lord
As it's messing up my life.
Already, I have lost my home,
My children and my life.
Yet, I know that I can't do it
Without special help from you,
I'd appreciate you sending
a friend to see me through.
It's often hard to show it
When I feel so much defeat
So, I'll wait here for your help, Lord
To get me off this street.

As a result of the abuse she had experienced, this young woman did not become a criminal but rather turned to alcohol to try to forget her history and her loss. She was a lost and rejected soul. Her desperation and hopelessness are beautifully expressed in what she scratched on a piece of paper and handed to us.

Worldwide Evidence

Over 45 years of research into parental acceptance and rejection has been conducted by Ronald P. Rohner, Ph.D. A leading expert on multicultural parental acceptance/rejection and its effect upon the offspring, he is the founder of the University of Connecticut's **Ronald and Nancy Rohner Center for the Study of Parental Acceptance and Rejection** and the author of several books and numerous articles on this subject. Dr. Rohner calls upon nearly 2,000 studies among every major ethnic group in the United States, and several hundred societies worldwide, to report the implications and results of rejection upon children and upon adults who were rejected in childhood.

From an article compiled by several of the center's staff, which reports the findings of multiple research projects, come five conclusions. The paper itself is prepared for academia, but the five conclusions can easily be understood:

> *Nearly 200 studies suggest that children's feelings of being loved, cared about, wanted and appreciated probably have greater developmental consequences than any other single parental influence. Improved messages of parental love appear to be the most salient (significant) route through which effective parenting techniques contribute to healthy child development.*

1. Extensive study in every major ethnic group within the U.S. and in several hundred societies worldwide reveals a common meaning structure that children use to determine if they are loved (accepted). Culture and ethnicity shape the specific words and behaviors that carry these concepts, but children everywhere seem to organize their perceptions around these dimensions of parenting:

- Warmth and affection
- Hostility and aggression
- Indifference and neglect
- Undifferentiated rejection (cannot be observed by others, but is felt by child)

Every cultural and ethnic group has ways to communicate love, and children readily recognize these ways.

2. Compared to children who feel loved, children who feel rejected are at greater risk for developing specific forms of psychological maladjustment. In turn, these feelings and behaviors often become associated everywhere with:

- Behavior problems, conduct disorders, delinquency, and perhaps adult criminality
- Depression and depressed affects
- Substance (drug and alcohol) abuse—among other problems

3. The vast majority of studies testing the major postulates of PARTheory's (Parental Acceptance/Rejection Theory) Personality Sub-theory show that children who experience themselves to be rejected also display a constellation of personality dispositions—a syndrome.

- Hostility
- Aggression
- Passive-aggression
- Emotional unresponsiveness
- Immature dependence or defensive independence
- Impaired self-esteem
- Impaired self-adequacy
- Emotional instability
- Negative worldview

4. Evidence from PARTheory research documents the fact that fathers' love-related behaviors often have as strong or even stronger implications for children's social-emotional development than do mothers' love-related behaviors. For example, fathers' love-related behavior (or the love-related behavior of the other significant male caregivers) is often as strongly—or more so—associated with offspring's sense of health and well-being in childhood and later adulthood, as is mother's. Paternal (fathers') rejection, however, is sometimes more strongly associated than mothers' rejection with such negative developmental outcomes as depression and depressive affect, conduct problems and substance abuse, to mention but three outcomes.

Rohner, Khaleque and Cournoyer. For a review of the entire document, refer to the Center for the Study of Parental Acceptance and Rejection at the University of Connecticut.

Simply Stated:

1. Being loved, cared about, wanted and accepted is the single most important factor in the development of healthy children.

2. In every culture, children recognize whether or not they are loved and accepted by the same means: warmth and affection, hostility and aggression, indifference and neglect, or undifferentiated rejection.

3. Children who are rejected are at a greater risk for psychological maladjustment.

4. Children who feel rejected display negative personality behaviors.

5. Fathers' love-related behaviors have as strong or even stronger an influence on children than do mothers' love-related behaviors.

Rejection is real, and loitering in the shadows is a frightening nightmare! For those who felt it in childhood, it is a way of thinking, feeling, and predicting the outcome of all relationships in the future. Rejected people look for rejection everywhere, and if they don't find it, they manufacture it in their minds or display behaviors guaranteed to get them rejected. Rejection feels normal to them. It's what they are used to experiencing, and they busy themselves seeking what feels normal and, in a strange sense, comfortable.

Chapter Seven

Is Physical Health Affected?

For some time we have taught that wounds experienced in childhood not only cause negative emotional consequences but also negatively influence our physical health. Years ago, Dr. Hans Eysnek and his colleagues from the University of London showed that chronic, unmanaged stress—of the emotional and mental variety—was six times more predictive of coronary heart disease and cancer than cigarette smoking or high blood pressure. Many people have questioned us regarding this and have felt that we were way off base, but later science has proven Dr. Eysnek to be correct!

In a book by an author whom we respect very highly and whose classes we have sat in, we have found scientifically founded evidence that shows Eysnek's assertion to be valid—and, indeed, even more evidence has been discovered to that effect.

A scientist by the name of Dr. Vincent Felitti is quoted in this book, which is entitled *Born to Love*. It is written by Dr. Bruce D. Perry, founder of the Child Trauma Academy, and Maia Szalavitz, a science journalist.

The following words are from Dr. Feletti's article entitled "The Relationship of Adverse Childhood Experiences to Adult Health: *Turning gold into lead*":

> *The question of what determines adult health and well-being is important to all countries. The Adverse Childhood Experiences (ACE) Study 1 is a major American research project that poses the question of whether, and how, childhood experiences affect adult health decades later. This question is being answered with the ongoing collaboration of Robert Anda, MD at the Centers for Disease Control (CDC) and the*

cooperation of 17,421 adults at Kaiser Permanente's Department of Preventive Medicine in San Diego, California. Kaiser Permanente is a multispecialty, prepaid, private health insurance system or Health Maintenance Organization [HMO]. The findings from the ACE Study provide a remarkable insight into how we become what we are as individuals and as a nation. They are important medically, socially, and economically. Indeed, they have given us reason to reconsider the very structure of primary care medical practice in America.

The ACE Study reveals a powerful relationship between our emotional experiences as children and our physical and mental health as adults, as well as the major causes of adult mortality in the United States. It documents the conversion of traumatic emotional experiences in childhood into organic disease later in life. How does this happen, this reverse alchemy, turning the gold of a newborn infant into the lead of a depressed, diseased adult? The Study makes it clear that time does not heal some of the adverse experiences we found so common in the childhoods of a large population of middle-aged, middle class Americans. One does not "just get over" some things, not even fifty years later.

Read the rest of the report in Appendix I.

How amazing it is that the entire physical body would be affected by the abusive experiences of childhood! It would be easy to comprehend how the brain and the mind would be affected, but this new information is very exciting and explains the lack of good health in many people.

Let's go back now to the people we have written about in this book. Do you suppose that any of them have experienced adverse childhood effects?

RON

Ron was always a "healthy horse," and he would brag about his health and about how his outlook on life had determined that he would never get sick. Whenever anyone close to him was ill, or if they were suffering from allergies, he would say that their illness was "all in their head," causing others to feel inadequate for being unable to think away their illness. His healthiness persisted until he was in his 40s, when high blood pressure began to meddle with his mindset. He assumed, and rightly so, that stress in his life was contributing to his dramatic increase in blood pressure. The change was so dramatic that it was life-threatening: He was on the verge of a stroke! He had experienced a short episode of elevated BP once before, which diminished when he was able to make a career change. But this time his doctor told him, "Get rid of the stress, or die." He chose to sell his business, which was far too demanding, and return to a less hectic way of life.

At that time, Ron was 54 years of age. We were in a career that was exciting to both of us and which gave us the privileges of being creative and traveling a great deal. Our horizons had been broadened. We felt that we were helping people to feel better about themselves and to undo the ravages of wounds they had experienced. This bolstered our energy and our outlook. This career path still continues to a limited degree; we are now semi-retired. It is still creative and exciting to us, and it allows us some travel and continued work with individuals, couples and families. However, Ron has developed the dreaded Parkinson's disease. As of yet there is no cure, but there are methods for lessening the effects and pushing back the clock for more time.

In Dr. Bruce Perry's book *Born For Love*, we read that Ron's Parkinson's can be related to his earliest days of life. You can be sure that when I (Nancy) read it, it was very upsetting to me that the way Ron was treated in his earliest days, weeks and months may have contributed to what he is dealing with presently.

The release of endogenous opioids (oxytocin) and dopamine (neurotransmitter) is an aspect of the stress response, a part *of the cycle that helps restore the system to balance. There has to be a biological way to ensure that we will connect with others: <u>these chemicals and the pleasures they produce are the glue that bonds us.</u>*

Pages 29-30.

One of the most important architectural features of the brain is a set of neurotransmitter systems that originates in the central, lower areas of the brain. These systems include norepinephrine, dopamine and serotonin neurons that send projections up to virtually every part of the brain and down to the autonomic nervous system that regulates the heart, lung, gut, pancreas, skin and rest of the body. It is no surprise, then, that these are some of the most important components of the stress response system.

Ibid. Pages 37-38.

. . . it is the attentive, attuned and nurturing care of a baby's primary caregiver that begins to shape and regulate these developing stress response systems.

Ibid. Page 38.

Patterned, repetitive activity is, in fact, necessary to all kinds of learning—whether building the neural systems needed to manage stress or trying to build stronger muscles.

Ibid. Page 38.

Dr. Perry goes on to show that in lab animals (moles), if you block dopamine or oxytocin, no bonding occurs.

Failing to experience normal bonding changes the oxytocin system. And this can have terrible consequences, particularly with regard to the ability to find comfort and pleasure in loving and being loved by others. Lack of nurture directly affects key brain regions that create the experience of joy, desire and motivation.

Ibid. Page 133.

Dr. Perry also reports that those with less nurturing mothers are prone to seek nurturing from addictions to drugs or alcohol. He states:

> *Your early environment—specifically the amount of nurturing you receive—can determine how much pleasure you get from nurturing, from being nurtured, and from drugs. This is how nurture implements nature.*

Ibid. Page 134.

One of the results of sexual abuse is obesity. In consulting with many women who experienced childhood sexual abuse, I (Nancy) have noticed that the majority have had and continue to suffer with weight gain. As a victim myself, I have fought with this for a lifetime, and the onset of my "fight" corresponds with the timing of my sexual abuse as a child. Somehow, overeating became a comfort to me, along with thumb-sucking, until I was 16 and heading for college. The additional side effect of weight gain and thumb-sucking was emotional abuse from friends and family. It is often the case that the abused are re-abused because of the methods of comfort they have adopted.

GEORGE

George was Ron's brother—remember? He was the scapegoat of the family, and he was regularly beaten with his father's razor strap while his mother encouraged Dad to beat him harder and longer.

George's life after childhood was one of repeated incarcerations. In fact, he spent more of his years behind bars than he did outside of them. During his first marriage, he fathered a son and a daughter. When the little girl was just 14 months old, she was scalded to death from hot steam that came out of the faucet and into her bath water. George was devastated to lose his little girl, and, blaming his wife for the accident, his marriage with her ended shortly thereafter.

After several years in and out of prison, he met a young woman who was to become wife number two. It was during that time that George reached out to God in an attempt to straighten out his life, but he could not maintain a connection with Him. The obstacle that stood in his way was the history of his torturous treatment in his childhood home, which haunted him and distanced him from God. He married MaryAnn and conceived two sons with her; but then, unable to stay responsible and committed, he abandoned his wife and children, leaving them penniless and hungry. Such a capacity for positive experiences had never been developed in this young man. The pain of his physical and emotional abuse was so great that he was unable to learn from positive models, if he had any, the qualities he needed to be a healthy husband and parent. Those early, formative years became the huge obstacle that stood in the way of his receiving enough light to dispel the shadows. So not only George, but also everyone connected with him, lived in the shadow of his pain.

It became necessary for George to have a six-place coronary bypass surgery; and, because he had no place to go and no family or friends to take him in, he recovered from that while sitting in a bar all night. Later a four-place bypass was necessary, and then major surgery and reconstruction was needed for cancer in his jaw and face. Again he recovered alone. It was then that Ron found him and paid him the visit that initiated his turnaround.

Some may say, "Well, he should have just manned up and gotten over the childhood junk," but George was just not able to do that without assistance. That ability depends to a large degree on the brain gift of an individual, and George's gift to his brain just wasn't in the one powerful quadrant that could have pulled off that feat. Very few people can recover on their own without someone walking alongside them who is knowledgeable and caring.

George, Ron's older brother, was always the largest of the three sons. He was 6 feet, 6 inches tall and took size 15 EEE shoes!

He got to the point where he was far too overweight, as he no doubt comforted himself with food.

After several more years in prison and repeated but unsuccessful attempts to "get it together" with God, George was wandering like a lost puppy. After his mother's death, George disappeared from the family for 12 years. We discovered that he had told people that he had no family. However, Ron was compelled to find his older brother, fearing that he would die alone and feeling abandoned by his family. In actuality, the family liked it this way, because if he wasn't around them, he wouldn't be stealing from them.

Through the help of a friend, Ron managed to find George. He flew out to see him, taking our books and tapes in which his life story was told. George read, listened, and watched, and as a result he was able for the first time to see light at the end of the tunnel. He was able to get in touch with the genuinely loving and soft heart that God had given him, and he became a blessing to his community up until his death.

Was George able to re-connect with his three sons? No. He had no idea how to be a father because emotionally he was extremely wounded, and he never matured to the place where he could be a strong and loving father figure to his sons. Was George able to connect with God before his death? We think so, because the dramatic change in his life, going from a taker to a giver, demonstrates that a transformation had taken place.

Fathers stand in the place of God to their children when they are little. Children do not have the capacity to understand such a concept—that is, something they cannot see. And who in the world would want to worship or have a relationship with a God whose attributes were like his father's? George had never really matured emotionally; he had never gone past the hurts that stacked up against him and prevented him from seeing the light of God's love and acceptance.

WE CAN LEARN FROM RON'S SITUATION

Recently, we sought out the help of a world-renowned physician located in Naples, Florida, Dr. David Perlmutter. He is a board-certified neurologist who specializes in treating people with Parkinson's disease. As you have already read, Ron has been diagnosed with this disease, and we had heard and read about the nearly miraculous results this doctor is seeing in Parkinson's patients who are being treated with glutathione. Once in his office, we got to the "bottom line" rather quickly. He interviewed Ron regarding his childhood, and Ron was very upfront and honest about the abuses he had endured. We also shared that we were working to provide assistance to those whose current behaviors are hurtful to themselves and others; those who feel angry, fearful, depressed, and worthless; and those who are addicted to mind-altering substances or behaviors that do not serve them well. The doctor said, "I have something for you"; and he went to his large bookcase to retrieve a book he had co-written with a psychologist. He agreed with Dr. Bruce Perry about childhood wounds' being a causative agent for Parkinson's and other neurodegenerative diseases.

In the work we do, we regularly encounter people who are carrying a heavy load of pain—a cross, as it were. The pain they carry is usually discovered to have occurred in the womb and during the early years of life when character (thoughts and feelings) is being formed. After reading the stories of those in this book whose lives were negatively impacted by the wounds they received, please be aware that as life progresses, many of them will develop neurodegenerative diseases such as Alzheimer's, Parkinson's, ALS (Lou Gehrig's disease), fibromyalgia, and multiple sclerosis. Others will develop coronary artery disease, affecting their blood pressure and heart function. Cancer has also been shown to have emotional wounds as causative agents. The body's immune system is compromised by these wounds, according to Dr. Perlmutter.

Usually these diseases show up with age, but they have begun, according to Dr. Perlmutter and other specialists, long before the symptoms appear. Those who develop neurodegenerative diseases do so because the mitochondria of the brain's neurons begin to function poorly and die. Mitochondria form the powerhouse or energy of the cells (neurons), and they supply energy to the body.

Read carefully what the authors of *Power Up Your Brain* say about your beginnings:

> *For the sake of survival, a child needs to develop an instinctive sense for potentially threatening situations. This is why, early in life, we develop aversions and fears in association with events and experience that, rightly or wrongly, we perceive as dangerous. A great many of these aversions developed while we were still inside our mother's womb.*
>
> *A flood of stress hormones crosses the placental barrier and informs the fetus of exactly the mood and feeling state that its mother is in. If the mother is happy, the fetus is joyous. If the mother feels safe and loved, this message is registered by the fetus, who also feels safe and loved. If the mother considers terminating the pregnancy, neural networks in the fetal brain are coded for fear as it may intuitively perceive that its life is in danger.*
>
> *It is in this formative pre-natal time that a large percentage of the neural pathways in our brain develop, biasing the way we see and feel the world, and determining our personality. These biases are later reinforced by the codes of conduct and the emotional repertoire that we learned from our parents.*
>
> *Until about age seven, the human brain is a fertile field, absorbing information, first from the mother's placenta, then from a host of external post-birth influences.*
>
> *During those early years of life, the child's brain is like a digital recorder set on constant record. Or, measured with electroencephalogram (EEG), the brain wave frequency of a child from birth to age two is in the delta range, which is*

also the frequency of the brain waves in a sleeping adult. The brain wave frequency for a child from 2 to 6 is in the theta range, which is what an adult experiences in a state of imagination or reverie or wild dreaming. Only into young adult does a child's brain become fully adult-functional, operating in the higher frequencies of alpha or beta wave ranges. In other words, a child under 7 years of age basically functions in a hypnotic trance or dream state, which allows that digital recorder in the brain to gather information and form neural pathways appropriate for the youngsters' environment without the filtering and interference of logic and reasoning from the neocortex.

Then, between the ages of 7 and 16, something quite the opposite happens. We take ourselves out of the record mode and start playing around with delete/erase mode instead. During the years of adolescence our brains eliminate over 80 percent of the interconnections between neurons, in a process known as synaptic pruning.

Why? Because we have learned what's happening in the environment around us. We have a pretty good idea of whom to trust and whom not to trust, who provides food and hugs, and who inflicts pain and punishment. And so we no longer need to gather data from all possible sources, explore behavioral options, and seek alternative ways of experiencing the world.

Shortly after our late teens, we become bound by tradition, anchored by the way things have always been, and entrenched in the belief that everything will remain the same even as the world changes around us. Our world-view is set—not in stone, but in the neuronal networks of the brain. And while these neuronal networks communicate, chemically and electrically, we experience them as emotions.

Pages 45-47.

RICKY

As a result of the wounds that Ricky experienced in his early life—wounds that we know had been experienced in at least two generations before him on both sides of the family—he sought out methods to create some kind of pleasure in life. This is what the brain normally seeks. Who in their right mind would gravitate toward greater pain, we ask? Well, wait a minute!

Individuals who have been severely rejected, according to their perception, or who have been the victims of sexual abuse, often do seek greater pain because their ability to feel pain has been compromised as the result of the abuse. Some cut themselves with sharp objects. Some pierce multiple parts of their bodies with studs and rings. Others endure the sting of tattoos being drawn on various parts of their body. Actually, while many think that these are outward symbols of toughness and a "you stay away from me" attitude, they are really screams for help to get beyond the initial pain they experienced in childhood. "Pay attention to me! Can't you see that I'm in pain? If I can feel pain, then I know that I have selfhood and that I exist."

While Ricky chose tattoos and dangerous exploits in what some would label a "death wish," the greater damage was done to him from a method designed to help one forget, numb, and assuage pain: drinking alcohol. The very sad thing is that alcohol addiction is a slow death, as Ricky discovered when he had his brain scanned. Without healing, what would be in his future? According to Rick's report from the well-respected Amen Clinic, he would fall victim to Alzheimer's disease at a young age.

Are All the Wounded Stuck?

Absolutely not! What you have read is basically the diagnostic process of understanding where you may find yourself and how you have gotten to where you are, but the treatment comes very soon. You see, one has to know what they are dealing with before some pill or treatment can be prescribed. You can't fix what you can't see.

In this case, we are saying that what you first need is knowledge. Once you have it, you can apply it to yourself piece by piece. If it applies to you, then you can begin the process of removing the negative emotions from old wounds. As you do that, your pain begins to diminish until it is finally, hopefully, alleviated. It is the negativity in your memories of the past that drive your behaviors—conscious or subconscious. With the negative trash removed, your behaviors can begin a transformation.

Many of the ways we have used to survive our wounds have been our attempts at experiencing pleasure. Food, accomplishments that have created undue stress, drugs, tobacco, alcohol, addictions of all kinds—these have been our attempts to fix what hurt early on in our lives. Those "fixes" have, in most cases, only wounded us further. But there is HOPE for your future. Knowledge is power! And the truth is: "If you are teachable, you are fixable!"

Chapter Eight

Putting It Together

From what you have learned so far, you are discovering that multiple factors combine to make a person feel, think and behave as they do:

*   The influences of our time in the womb

*   The particular quadrant of our brain that is most highly oxygenated

*   During our earliest days, weeks and months, the way our parents connected with us on the emotional and physical levels

*   The feeling of rejection—the most severe wound anyone can receive, especially when it comes from parents, grandparents, and those in closest relationship to us

*   Additional wounds we experience before our characters (thoughts and feelings) are completely formed (conception to the end of the seventh year of life)

*   <u>Parental behaviors:</u>

    *   FATHERS stand in the place of God to their children and have three of the characteristics of God, if they are healthy men: provider, protector and priest. If the father is absent, as in the cases of Ron, Sam, Rick, Maria, and Nancy (during the first four years of her life), then, to that child, God is absent.

    *   If the father is harsh, cruel, critical, or dismissive, then God is too!

- If the father will not connect on an intimate (in-to-me-see) level with his children, then, to the child, God won't connect.

- MOTHERS are to be compassionate, concerned care-givers—also characteristics of God. How can a boy or a girl connect with God positively when his or her birth mother didn't care, wasn't concerned, and didn't understand (was not compassionate), or when she was plagued with her own issues? So that connection with God is frightening—if it ever happens!

So many people tell the wounded that God is their answer. Know what? They are RIGHT!! BUT how do you put trust and faith in God when you have never experienced them early on through your parents?

We can quote scripture from Genesis to Revelation about the loving Heavenly Father, but, without ever having experienced the unconditional, "not-dependent-on-performance" love of a mother or father, how can one even comprehend what love is? Most individuals, like those whose stories you have read, do not know the true meaning, nor have they ever experienced the comfort and joy, of a loving relationship. Thus they view all people through the dark glasses, or the shadows, of their previous experiences, especially those in their earliest character-forming hours, days, weeks and months.

The behaviors of others are predicted by what we have already experienced in life. We watch for signs of how they will treat us. Take, for example, the individual whose brain gift is basal right. This person has the incredible ability to observe facial expressions, tones of voice, and body language, and from them predict what someone else is thinking, feeling and planning. They know enough to run and hide in order to avoid a conflict that is life-threatening to them. The frontal right will usually diffuse a tense situation with a joke or some "off-the-wall" behavior. The basal left will run to their closet, so to speak, to hide, or will perform by organizing and structuring in order to diminish fear. The frontal left will be the one who "puts up their dukes" and fights. Basal rights can also be quite feisty if they have been so conditioned in their early years.

Unless you've been raised in a warm and loving home with a whole and healthy mother and father who taught you about the things of God, including His love and concern, it is difficult to believe what you have not experienced. The obstacle of your past life experiences stands in the way of your being able to receive the full light of God's love and caring.

WHAT DOES IT TAKE?

Each person follows his or her own path to God, but in nearly every case there are certain conditions that prompt one to reach out for Him. The steps to spirituality are colored by life experiences, to be sure! Perhaps you know someone whose life demonstrates something beyond what you've ever known—a love, a willingness to listen, a caring and compassionate spirit—and you would like to emulate that person. Maybe someone approached you when you found yourself in some sort of "tight spot" and offered you a Bible or some other reading material that kick-started an interest in religion or spiritual things. Maybe you found yourself in a place where you were just fed up with life as it was, and something just told you that calling on God might help.

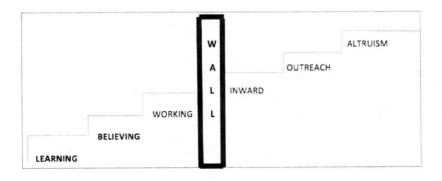

All along in your life, you have been **LEARNING**—from your development in the womb to the present moment. You have learned through the filter, or the glasses, of everything that has occurred around you and directly or indirectly affected you. You have even learned through movies and television, and through what you might have absorbed in school and in books you might have read. Your feelings about what you've experienced have tweaked your memories and have become the "gospel according to you."

What you have seen, heard, smelled, tasted, touched and felt has become part of your **BELIEF SYSTEM.** Accuracy has nothing to do with this. If you believe or perceive it, you receive it as your truth! What you have learned in school, in church, at home, or on the playground either has become part of your beliefs or has been tossed out by you as unbelievable. It has become a cornerstone of the way you lead your life. Your decisions are based on what you believe. Perhaps you believe that God doesn't exist or that he is sitting far away, unconcerned about you. If so, you learned that from your earliest experiences.

Perhaps you felt unloved even though your parents did the best they could to convey their love to you. As a result, you grew up honestly believing that whatever they did or didn't do was not good enough, and maybe you have chosen to distance yourself from them. It could be that you knew only what you observed as a child and not the whole story behind what you saw.

As you were starting your school life and the **WORKING** that you did to accomplish the tasks of "reading, writing and arithmetic," all you did, and the way you did it, was a result of what you had learned and believed. In Ron's schooling, he never did accomplish much in elementary and secondary school. Actually, he quit high school at the beginning of the tenth grade, certain that he could not learn. His father, a very frightening character, tried to pound his spelling words into him, but to no avail. Memorization was impossible for him. But why?

Abuse dumbs down a victim. While the abuse is going on at home, a child is simply trying the best he can to survive. The human brain will use all of its energy and all of its resources to see that it and the person to whom it belongs will survive at all costs. In his difficult family situation, Ron used all of his energy to survive not being wanted. Once his brother came along, it took an even greater supply of energy to watch the attention his brother received but that he did not enjoy. In Ron's case, survival meant taking the things he wanted because his family would give but then take them away. This was true even for the simple necessities of life. When it came to shoes, for example, Ron's father would rant and rave at the shoe store when the salesman said that he needed larger shoes. How does a child handle a parent who screams obscenities at a salesman because his son's feet have grown?

The truth is that every individual works at surviving life. Even adored or privileged children have issues to overcome and negatives to survive. Giving a child everything he wants causes him to think that the world owes him. Not learning how to accomplish or work for things, or how to save up from little jobs to buy that special toy, delaying gratification until the item can be purchased, produces an adult who is sure that the world owes him. His self is on the throne, and the needs of others are ignored. His self becomes primary in order to survive!

THE WALL: At some point in life, every individual hits a wall! Usually this occurs in one's 30s, when the adrenaline needed to keep the lid on the garbage can of painful emotions starts decreasing and the individual feels the need to blow up, explode, or collapse. Life seems to be dealing devastating blows all at once, and the ability to cope is minimal.

What then? Have you been at the wall? Perhaps you're there now. Maybe you are wondering why life is crumbling around you and all hell seems to be breaking loose. Are you having a hard time understanding it? Are you angry with your parents or others and blaming them for the mess you're in? Are you blaming

God for not coming to your aid when you snap your fingers? Maybe that's why you are at the wall: to be taught a valuable life lesson. It's certainly happened to Ron and me numerous times!

It is at the wall where major decisions are made! Those decisions change the course of one's life for good (positive change) or for not so great (negative change). Here you feel like you've been banging your head against the wall for an eternity—and perhaps you have! Have others endeavored to help you, but you have turned the other way? Honestly, now: Has God endeavored to "get to you," and somehow you know it, but you just can't bring yourself to pay attention?

You see, the learning, believing, and working apply to Christians as well as non-Christians. When we learn in childhood that we have to perform for acceptance, we apply that to God and keep working for Him, like the devil; but somehow we feel that the acceptance we crave just doesn't get satisfied.

Both in Christian life and in normal everyday life, we find ourselves on a merry-go-round of learning > believing > working, and back to learning again. It's as if we think that the more facts we have in our arsenal, the stronger we will be. We decide to believe these facts and then live our day-to-day existence working so hard to prove that we are OK—OK as human beings, and OK with God. But at the wall, nothing is OK. That life-changing decision we spoke about, the one we make at the wall, either gets us stuck there or allows us to open the door and enter a new experience. This new experience requires:

- an in-depth look at oneself

- an honest acknowledgement of the merry-go-round you've been on

- a willingness to accept the help to continue on the path toward wholeness, emotionally and spiritually

The look in the mirror, so to speak, is not always an easy task or a pleasant sight. We look around and see the circumstances in which we find ourselves, and we do our best to find someone else to blame! It's much easier to look in a real mirror, grab a comb, fix our hair or shave, and then feel better. But this mirror is a whole different ball game! A comb or a razor won't fix what we see! Honestly answering questions about your past will!

WHAT'S BEYOND THE WALL?

INWARD: Looking inward is the first thing we do beyond the wall. It is a self-examination, a deep look at your beginnings and how those early life experiences have affected your life. It's telling yourself the truth, maybe for the very first time. It is NOT about blaming your parents, because, remember, they were the products of their parents going back four generations. Now, if our parents do deserve some responsibility for how they treated us, don't lie to yourself or sugar-coat the truth; but be willing to acknowledge that they were no doubt wounded too, and they just passed on to us what they themselves experienced.

Remember my (Nancy's) story about my father, his mother, and her father, and how all of that impacted the way my father parented me? If you were wounded by parents, count on their having been wounded as children too. Remember, I was expected to be perfect but just couldn't meet up to my dad's expectations. So what do you suppose I did to my daughters? I expected them to be perfect—not so much to please me, but rather to please my parents so that my parents would accept me as a mother. And this is the way it has been since the Garden of Eden: The sins of the fathers have been passed on to the children down to the third and fourth generations.

Here in the inward portion of your path to wholeness is where you could use the assistance of a supportive small group. In *The Journey* or *Binding the Wounds*, the small group programs for recovery, five or six people meet together and form a supportive group. They go through an actual program to go from being stuck to becoming unstuck.

While you are in the process of looking inward, you will move to the next step of **REACHING OUTWARD**. Others will begin to notice the changes in you, and they will ask you about them and about what you're doing. Here you can testify about what you are learning about yourself, and here you can encourage others to open the doors in their own walls and step up to the process that begins to answer their life questions like nothing else can. You will find it hard to keep quiet about what you are learning and how you feel such positive internal changes taking place.

The last step in the process is **ALTRUISM,** the experience of selflessness where you feel empathy for the hurts you see in others, and you begin to reach out to them, sacrificially being of benefit however and whenever you can. Your self steps off the throne, and the need to benefit others becomes primary.

ACTUALLY, we do not just go from one step to another and then stop at altruism. We continue to learn, form beliefs, and work on ourselves and for the benefit of others. And when we reach the wall, we go straight through the open door of introspection, outreach, and altruism. No longer are we on a self-defeating merry-go-round; we are now on a path of self-awareness, improvement, and benefitting others.

As we continue in this process, not only will we feel great emotional relief and spiritual connection, but our physical body will benefit as well.

Chapter Nine

Ron's Changes—How They Occurred

In the 1960s, state penitentiaries were daunting places at best. Ron was sentenced to six years in the Tennessee State Prison, a massive, walled compound that looked like a foreboding castle. As the prison bus drove onto the grounds of the prison, he noticed that the United States flag was not flying, and that signaled to him that this place would be very hard to handle. As it happened, the prisoners had rioted a week or two before Ron's arrival, and the warden had taken the matter very seriously, punishing prisoners in every way he could think of. He had actually confiscated all of their Bibles and had them dumped in a pile in the center of the "yard." Gasoline was dumped on them, and they were burned to bits.

Ron had been in another Tennessee prison six months or so before arriving at the state penitentiary, and there the abuse of the guards against prisoners was brutal. He had been sunburned so severely from working under the Tennessee summer sun that he could barely walk or see through the slits that his eyes had become. The result of his plea for an indoor pass got him solitary confinement in a 4' x 6' x 6' cold, damp box for six weeks. He had seen beatings so severe that one prisoner had one side of his face ripped open by a guard using his enormous keys.

There, Ron was young and arrogant, and he made a plan of escape and carried it out successfully. It was when he was picked up six months later for racking up a large hotel debt, and with no money to pay it, that authorities discovered that he was an escaped convict. He would serve time for that offense, too, at the "Big House."

It was a frightening place at best, and Ron knew he would have to make the best of it for six long years. He had learned how to fingerprint and classify fingerprints, and he had learned about photography at another prison. He had even developed the pictures of the escape from Alcatraz. So giving him a job in the classification center was easy for the warden, and a blessing for Ron.

Apart from his time spent working, confinement in his cell was required. Participation in any activity that would get him out of his cell helped him to feel less trapped. On Sundays there was a Catholic church service, so he attended to throw spitballs at the priest's back as he prepared Communion. Saturdays were boring until an announcement went up on the bulletin board that he passed in the chow line. It read that there would be a Saturday church service, and Ron signed up for that one, too. The guards made every effort to prevent him from going on Saturdays, but as providence would have it, and against all odds, he managed to attend.

Leonard Haswell was a father-like figure who came each Saturday from the outside and in time built up a congregation of 500 men in that prison. It wasn't what Haswell preached that finally made a dent in Ron's tough armor, but rather it was Haswell's arm around him as he called him "Son" that began to melt Ron's heart. For the first time in his life, he felt that he had value and that someone cared. This is what every human being needs—to belong—and it is one of the reasons that cliques and gangs exist and are so powerful. They are of great importance to those who are basically orphaned from their birth families. Being an orphan doesn't require that one's parents be absent. Mom and Dad can be physically present but emotionally detached, as was the case in Ron's life.

Little by little Ron began to read the Bible that Leonard had given to him as well as other inspirational books. He immersed himself in research into who God was and whether He cared about him. He attended church services every time they were held in the chapel, and he worked at making a decision as to which denomination he would join. Finally, on one Saturday afternoon, he was baptized into Haswell's church.

Ron served a total of 4½ years in prison and was let out early for good behavior. Officers from the state of Wisconsin were waiting for him outside the walls, and they took him back to Milwaukee to face old charges there. After awaiting trial in the county jail for three months, Ron and I met in the courtroom the day he was first released. Ours was an instant attraction; and, after a nine-month courtship, we married.

Two weeks after our wedding, Ron enrolled in college with a GED from the Navy and a recommendation from someone whose opinion mattered. Thus began the seven years it would take for him to get through college with a B.S. in theology and a minor in history. During those seven years, we struggled in every way! There was physical illness, the birth of two daughters who had to be born then or never, four surgeries, financial strain, and marital torment.

Human beings are attracted to their emotional equals, and that is why Ron and I were attracted to each other. His childhood filled with rejection and the absence of his mother early in life, together with my father's absence for my first few years and his subsequent rejection of me, made our wounds the perfect match. He placed me in the mother role and expected that I could fill the hole she had left in his heart. I was not enough to do that, and neither were the other women he was attracted to. I placed Ron in the father role and expected him to be what my father had not been, while at the same time hoping that the behaviors of our courtship would continue in marriage. What disappointment we both experienced, and what a recipe for disaster!

Ron's fear of loss caused him to control my every move to ensure that I would stay. I allowed his control because it was familiar to me. Our two girls were, unfortunately, caught in the middle. There were many intense arguments. He yelled and I cried. My crying made him angrier; and the angrier he got, the more desperate I became. There was even a time that he left for 24 hours and flew to Canada on his way to Europe. There he thought he could escape to a new life with no responsibilities and without this woman who was "causing him so much pain." His trip was cut short, however, because he decided to call and say good-bye. I asked when he was coming home, and somehow he felt the love in my voice and said, "I'll be home in the morning."

You might ask, "I thought Ron had found a relationship with God in prison. What happened to that?" Getting to know the Heavenly Father provides us with the power for change, but it does not erase our memories filled with negative emotions. It is those emotions that drive our behaviors and orchestrate our relationships. Ron says, "Even though I'd been released from the 'Big House,' I was still imprisoned in my mind. I was even longing to be back behind bars so that I could escape the torture of marriage. And what did that look like? It was love and acceptance that I was experiencing but had never known back when my thoughts and feelings were being formed. It felt abusive to me."

Finally, having graduated from college, Ron was assigned to two churches, and we moved into the parsonage to begin our dream life. But living in the parsonage did not wipe away those memories we both carried from childhood and from our earlier years of marriage. Standing in a pulpit did not erase the pain in Ron's heart but rather only increased it when parishioners treated him poorly. Rejection raised its ugly head again! Both of us worked hard, attempting to prove to ourselves and to others that we had worth and value. Of course, that feeling should have been developed in early childhood, but for us it was not. Often humans will do whatever it takes to prove that they are OK, or, conversely, to prove that they are worthless. In our situation, no amount of success in the ministry could assuage the pain in our hearts and our great need to feel accepted.

By the time we had been in the ministry for about five years and had moved to our second district of two churches, our marriage had severely deteriorated! We were headed for the divorce courts, and we both knew it. Yet somewhere in our deepest selves we knew that God had brought us together in a very miraculous way, and that God never changes his mind. In desperation, Ron decided to enroll in graduate school for a degree in marriage and family therapy. "If I can't fix mine," he thought, "maybe I can fix everyone else's broken relationships."

After his first class—Emotional Growth of the Family—he came home and demanded that I get dressed up and head with him to Boston. "Going to get you enrolled," he demanded, "because there will be NO hope after this class if you don't attend too." Dutifully I followed and was enrolled as a special student for that class. The next semester I enrolled full-time, and we both graduated with M.Ed. degrees in marriage and family therapy from Antioch University New England.

It was during our acquisition of knowledge at Antioch that we began our turnaround. We compared what we learned with what we read in the Bible, kept what matched and pitched what didn't. Major changes began to take place in us individually and as a couple. We began to work with congregants who needed help, and that just benefitted us in the process. We led seminars, preached sermons, and prepared to spend the rest of our lives helping others.

Ron has spent every day since he graduated from college at age 30 in ministry of some sort. Several pastoral assignments later, we continued our work and did family life for two states as well. In 1995 we accepted a call to Faith For Today, a television ministry. There was a real soft spot in Ron's heart for Faith For Today because, while he was in Nashville's "Big House," one of the courses he took was a correspondence Bible course from that ministry. For ten years we traveled from place to place, first in a motor home, then a converted bus, and finally mostly by air as our work spread internationally.

As I write we look forward to our 48th wedding anniversary on August 15th of 2013. We are more "together" now than we've ever been. Our love has deepened as we have put our hands to the work of self-examination that we needed. We looked at our histories, identified our wounds (many of them generational), and processed through the pain of them. We know each other intimately because we have shared in depth about every aspect of our lives.

Someone once said, "Our mess becomes our mission," and for us no truer words were ever spoken. Each day Ron is doing research and I am writing. We continue to counsel couples together. Ron works with men, I work with women, and we facilitate the recovery programs we have created: *Binding the Wounds* and *The Journey* for adults, *Created For Success* for married couples, and *Journey to Nai* for teens. As far as we are concerned, God has called us to this work; and until He stops us, we'll never quit. Occasionally we conduct a seminar here in the United States or Canada. Every time we do, we look into the eyes of hurting people who, churched or un-churched, really need to feel valuable, loved, and set free. As we teach, we watch them recognize their pain and perhaps identify it for the first time. We see the light of hope beginning to show on their faces as we leave them with a plan and a process for them to empty out their pain so that they can be filled with love.

THINK ON THIS . . .

There are only two basic experiences in life. We either live in FEAR or we live in LOVE. All of the negativity we experience, all of the behaviors that we adopt, are our attempts at survival. That's what the human brain is designed to do: see that you survive at all costs. Think about it for a minute. Eating, sleeping, bathing—all of the everyday exercises of your life are about survival. Smoking, drinking alcohol, or taking drugs; being inappropriately sexual, angry, depressed, or addicted to behaviors—all of these are survival techniques. They all stem from the FEAR of not being loved—not belonging—and are attempts at getting your needs met.

The human heart is designed for LOVE. "Wait a minute," you might say, "the heart beats to pump blood through your body!" That is true. But new science proves that the heart actually has a brain that is located at the heart's base. Remember the saying, *"I love you from the bottom of my heart?"* Well, that's just where the collection of neurons are—at the bottom of the heart. The heart is the first responder to stimuli coming to us from the outside world.

Let's use this example:

You are driving on a major highway at 70 mph, and you start around a huge bend in the road. On your left you see red lights flashing, then red and blue lights flashing and cars and trucks piled and mangled on the road ahead. Your heart begins to beat faster so that blood gets pumped to your extremities so that you can react. Your brain kicks in and tells you to slow down, so you put your foot on the brake. As you do, you see what appear to be several bodies covered with blankets lying in the road. You hear an ambulance behind you a distance away, and you realize that there has been a horrific accident. Your heart is still pounding, and now your brain has kicked in to react beyond your immediate survival. Now you are deciding whether you should stop in the breakdown lane to help or just slowly pass by.

If you are tuned in to being a helper or a first responder to crisis situations, you will pull off the road and offer assistance. If not, chances are that you will slowly drive by, if that's possible.

The message that came to you through your eyes went straight to your heart. Your heart sent the message to your brain's limbic system to determine whether this was a threat to you. Once your brain alerted you to use your brake and you saw the mess in the road up close, your heart slowed down and your prefrontal cortex (behind your forehead) decided whether you should stop to offer help or pass on by.

Often when we have been wounded early on in life, we refer to our survival brain and leave the heart alone. We are designed to have the heart and brain work in tandem, as a team. When we do, we can live more in a place of love than in one of reactionary fear.

Ron continues to learn, and so do I, that it is safe to refer to the heart. When we do, our marriage takes a giant step forward; but should we rely on our survival brains alone, our tendency is to isolate and distance ourselves from each other. There's really no enjoyment in that!

Chapter Ten

What About Sam?

Thoughts of the electric chair must have haunted Sam as he languished in Ohio's penitentiary. He no doubt wondered when the day would actually arrive that he would be served his last requested meal and then be escorted to the dreaded little room with the big, wooden, electrified chair.

As it happened, Sam had received spiritual counsel from the jail's chaplain, but the chaplain's words had not penetrated his hardened heart. One day two laymen from a local church who had heard of Sam's sentencing came to the jail and asked for permission to visit with him. Their request was denied with the excuse that he had already had spiritual counsel. Disheartened, the men did not leave but instead stayed for a while, perhaps hoping and praying that the officers would change their minds.

Soon they were told, "Oh, well, I guess it can't do any harm to let you go in to see him," and the guard then escorted them to Sam's cell.

Perfect approach or not, the men stood outside Sam's jail cell and preached to him a heartfelt sermon about the love of God and His desire to save souls. Their efforts were rewarded, as Sam said he would accept a Bible they said they would bring for him if he agreed to read it. They also offered to enroll him in a Bible correspondence course so that he could understand what he was reading. Sam agreed to this as well, and the next day one of the men returned with a Bible. This was not just any Bible: It was the one his little boy had just received for his birthday, and he wanted his Dad to give it to Sam. There was something about the kind sincerity of these two men that began to melt Sam's hard heart, causing him to accept their offers and embrace the Bible and the course.

William A. Fagal, the founder of Faith For Today and himself an ordained preacher, learned of Sam through the teachers at the Bible Course School. Pastor Fagal records his experience:

"My first contact with Sam was in April 1956. He originally was scheduled to die in February, but he had been given a stay of execution. Presenting my letter at the front office, I was told to wait while a check was made to make certain that I was the one to whom the warden had written. Finally a special guard was assigned to take me to Sam and to remain with me throughout the visit."

He wondered what he was doing in that tiny room, but he soon spotted a peephole in a door at the end of the "closet" through which he was being watched by yet another guard. As soon as this guard was sure that the door behind them was locked, he opened the door with the peephole, and they passed through. They then entered into a large room filled with cells, the place of maximum security in the innermost part of the prison.

Pastor Fagal noticed that a chair had been placed outside one of the cells, and he was told to go there and sit. The guard pulled up a chair about eight feet away where he could hear every word that would pass between them. In the cell, behind two sets of bars and a screen, sat a frail-looking prisoner whose face was filled with expectancy. I asked, "Are you Sam?" He replied, "I am Sam," and then proceeded to call me by name even though we had never met.

Through the correspondence course, the teachers and Pastor Fagal had detected quite a change in Sam, and Pastor Fagal wanted to visit to see if the change was as genuine as they had assumed at Faith For Today. Indeed it was, and even the warden had agreed on Sam's change in demeanor as he discovered his worth and value in God's eyes.

"Sam," I said, "it is hard to find you here and to meet you in this place, realizing why you are here and what lies in store for you."

He replied, "Pastor, don't feel sorry for me. I am the happiest man in the world."

The Pastor said, "What makes you say that, Sam?"

He answered, "When I was out there on the street, I had no hope." (He pointed vaguely outside.) "But since I've come here, I have found that Jesus Christ is my Saviour. Now I feel that what happens to me in the next few days doesn't matter. It is what happens to me 'over there' that counts, and I've got all the hope in the world for 'over there.' "

Sam said that in his first prayer he asked God for a pistol so he could shoot his way out of prison and then reform. For several days he suffered while considering the claims of Jesus Christ on his life, but in the end he asked for forgiveness for all his sins and placed his life in the hands of God. It was then he reported that peace had come to him, when he realized that God was in control.

Sam's execution was stayed again, but it was finally scheduled for November 26th. Pastor Fagal was notified by the warden that he could have a three-hour visit with Sam prior to his death. In his book, *By God's Grace, Sam*, the Pastor recalls that last visit, the execution, and the doctor's words: "Warden Alvis, sufficient current has passed through the body of Tannyhill to cause his death at 8:12 p.m."

Moments before Sam was escorted to the death chamber, he made another of his many attempts to relieve tension. He said, "There are not many men in the world at the present time who know that they have only one more minute of life. I guess I'm in quite a unique position." His attitude was one of thoughtfulness for those with him in that final, desperate hour.

One of Sam's concerns was for another death row inmate who was scheduled to die the following week. He was afraid that in the next week, without Sam's support, Earl would again sink into despair, so he made arrangements for visits to keep Earl bolstered and calm leading up to his execution. When we are relieved of the burden that we carry, we begin to see the burdens on others, and we reach out to be of assistance. This is called altruism.

Sam's great changes had also impacted his mother and stepfather, who came to see him once not long before his execution. During their visit they shared their commitments to Jesus Christ as their personal Saviour as well as their love for each other.

Sam was a changed man indeed. We know from science that there is an atmosphere—an aura, they call it—that surrounds us and reaches out toward others. That atmosphere, propelled by the heart, reaches out from four to ten feet, depending on the individual. It contains our conscious and subconscious thoughts and feelings, and either the LOVE or the FEAR we live in. Surely, Sam's aura was a blessing to everyone, even the guards and warden. Pastor Fagal recounts that he was extremely blessed and that he felt he was being ministered to during every visit with Sam.

Unfortunately, being transformed in the eyes of God and others does not undo our responsibility to suffer the consequences of poor choices we made earlier. Sam had to die for his sins to society and for taking the life of a waitress; but even as he took his last breath, he was alive with hope and a new life, including the promise of an eternal life to come.

Sam only lived to be 27 years of age, so we do not know of any physical effects of his childhood wounds as they often show up in our mid-life years. What we do know of are the emotional and behavioral effects that Sam suffered and foisted upon others.

If he were alive today, Sam would be 84 years old, and we would experience a man of wisdom who was indeed changed. Because of the love and kindness extended to him by two lay-men, and the grace and mercy of God that Sam found and ex-perienced, this change was able to come about. He would tell us how his childhood experiences had set the stage for his un-lawful and violent behaviors. He would sorrow over the ill treatment he dumped onto his two wives and several of his children.

He would give the glory of his transformation to two men whose hearts were filled with God's love and mercy, and who gave him the message that he was indeed loveable. He would revel in the transformative relationship he built with a loving God, which set him free while he was still imprisoned.

Sam felt, just like Ron, that one can be behind steel walls and yet feel totally free, or outside walking the streets feeling bound and imprisoned. The choice is ours!

Chapter Eleven

Catching Up With The Others

Hopefully, you have seen a pattern so far in the lives of Ron and Sam. That pattern is established while we are in the womb and during our first seven years of life. Remember, the brain collects information and tries to make sense of it during those years. Decisions are made that impact our worldview—the outlook, positive or negative, we all have.

We have indicated that the generations before us have an impact on who we are, how we think, how we feel, what we look like, and what our traditions and habits are like. For a number of years, Drs. Marcus Pembrey and Lars Bygren have studied the effects of previous generations on the people of today. Some of their work can be seen on the website www.Epigenie.com under these researchers' names. They have discovered that some of the effects we suffer in our physical bodies come from generations past. "It may not be what you eat that causes disease (diabetes) but what your grandmother or grandfather did or did not eat," they say. It has been found that the condition of the family's diet when your grandmother was in the womb of her mother determines whether or not you'll have diabetes today. Additionally, it's been discovered that what your grandfather ate or didn't get to eat due to famine during his puberty years determines whether or not you'll have diabetes today. Pembrey and Bygren report that a time of famine or plenty and its impact is different for males and females. For males it is during puberty when the sperm are multiplying, and for females it is while in the womb when all their eggs are formed, that it impacts those who come along several generations later.

Amazing, isn't it? But what of emotional issues and behaviors? Many have told me (Nancy) that I am a strong woman. I look back on that to recognize that the generations of women before me were also strong. My great-grandmother and great-aunt left England to bring my 18-year-old grandmother to America during World War I. The Lusitania, a passenger ship, had just been torpedoed and sunk with many lives lost. Undaunted, these three ladies, dressed in their long, corseted dresses, boarded a wooden cattle boat bound for this country. I call that brave and bold!

My grandmother met and married my grandfather in New Bedford, Massachusetts and not too long afterwards became pregnant with my mother. When Grandma was six months along, my grandfather came home from work at lunchtime to find her lying on the couch having convulsions from eclampsia—very high blood pressure. She was taken to the hospital and, while still convulsing, was anesthetized with chloroform. My mother was born by cesarean section and weighed only 2½ pounds. The doctor put my mother aside to save the life of my grandmother, knowing that my mother could not survive. But she did! Grandma took her home in a shoebox, and she was kept warm in the arms of Great-Grandma, Great-Aunt, and both of her parents. The old, black wood stove in the kitchen was a place of warmth as well. When the neighbors saw my tiny mother, they said that Grandma would never raise her to adulthood, but Grandma was determined!

My mother met and fell in love with my father, and they married. Two weeks after the wedding, he received the draft notice—World War II was beginning. My Dad was sent to Fort Preble, Maine for Basic Training and later Medic Training. It was during a 24-hour furlough that my mother became pregnant with me. When I was 14 months old, Dad was sent to Advanced Medic Training in Mississippi, and we accompanied him. It was during those three months that my mother became pregnant with my brother. Dad was then sent overseas and into the thick of the war, and we boarded the train back home to Connecticut.

During my mother's pregnancy, we would take the bus to see my father's father, who was dying of stomach cancer. Shortly after his death, my mother gave birth to my brother. She was quite ill, and they remained in the hospital for a couple of weeks. On day ten, an accident occurred in the nursery that took the life of my brother. What a tragedy! My mother came back home without little Jimmy, and she endured the loss and the grieving without my father's support. It was during a time in the war when wives were not allowed to know where in Europe their husbands were. Each day she watched as a sergeant came to town to inform a family of the death of a son or husband, and she worried that he might approach her.

My mother was a brave and tough woman, just like her mother and Grandma before her. Yet she had the softest and most tender heart ever. At age 51 she had a major heart attack and was not expected to survive, but instead she lived to age 85 and took care of both her parents until their deaths. I do have a heritage of women who have loved their families enough to suffer and sacrifice for them, and for that I am blessed.

WHAT ABOUT RICK?

What you have just read about generational physical and emotional health and its impact on us relates well to Rick's story. Recently we have discovered information about his mother's and grandmother's backgrounds that shows that the rejection he feels on a daily basis has not come from his experience alone but also from lives at least two generations before his.

Rick's grandmother was sent to a convent to live due to family trauma—the deaths of both her parents. All the children were separated into different places. Even though they had their parents for a brief time, all these children were orphaned to others or to the convent, so emotional connections were non-existent.

When Rick's mother was little, her mother gave her to one of her sisters to raise. Mary's mother lived across the street with her husband and his children, and she seldom saw or related with her daughter. Mary's mother bore other children with that husband, but she did not take Mary to live with them.

Would you consider both Mary and her mother orphans? They may have lived at home with one or both parentsfor a time during their early childhood, but they were "farmed out to other places" when it became inconvenient for them to stay. This is how it was with Rick. While he wasn't farmed out, he was not really a priority to his parents. Considering the facts that his father left when he was only two and that his mother had to farm him out while she was working to provide for the family, Ricky was left to "fend for himself" both physically and emotionally. Other relatives such as aunts or cousins are not the same as parents, and the child knows the difference and feels the abandonment. This can be the case even with loving stepparents.

The following report taken from an article at Softpedia.com describes the results of studies on orphans:

> *People with orphan spirits look normal and often are high achievers, but there's a hole in their heart and they hunger for acceptance. But they're plagued by orphan-like thoughts like, "Nobody loves me. I don't really matter. I have to perform to get attention or love," says Seth Barnes.*

> *The average IQ score in the general population is around 100. The below average score is probably due to the fact that intelligence is significantly influenced by what the child experiences in early life. "Many children raised in institutions are characterized by a variety of risk factors known to be associated with risk of psychiatric disorders," says Charles Zeanah of Tulane University in New Orleans. "That includes impoverished families of origin, limited prenatal care, prenatal exposure to alcohol and other drugs, as well as social and material deprivation after birth."*

> *However, the scientists don't understand exactly what causes this difference between girls and boys. Why do girls respond better to foster care, in terms of cognitive development? Is this difference caused by what happens in institutionalized*

care or do foster parents tend to treat boys and girls differently, for example being more talkative with girls and thus boosting their verbal skills?

"The girls placed in foster care do much better in terms of their IQ scores compared with boys," said Nathan Fox of the University of Maryland. "It's a very interesting finding. One wouldn't expect it [the sex difference] at all," said Seth Pollak, a developmental psychopathologist at the University of Wisconsin.

One possible answer was given by Zeanah. He studied emotional and behavioral disorders among fostered and institutionalized children and found that boys were more affected by behavioral disorders (such as hyperactivity and aggression) while girls were more likely to suffer from emotional disorders (such as anxiety and depression). In the same time, his team found that there was no difference between children in foster care or institutional care in case of the frequency of behavioral disorders, but on the other hand foster care tended to help in case of emotional problems.

"Girls are much more responsive to placement in foster care and have their [psychiatric] symptoms ameliorated more than boys," Zeanah notes.

The scientists discovered that psychiatric disorders were 3.5 times more common among institutionalized children than among children in normal family care.

As you've already read, Rick's father left when Rick was two, and his mother was left to feed and clothe and support her son. Her angst and her frustration from being abandoned and overwhelmed were often dumped onto Ricky when he was a child. She remarried, and that stepfather was cruel to Rick. They divorced and she remarried again, but by this time Ricky was mostly out of the house, living life on his own and away from the confusion of his many stepfathers.

How interesting and freeing it is to look back upon those who came before us. One would think that Rick's attitude toward his mother would change given the information available about her history. But consider the above report and the difficulty men find in being without their mother present both physically and emotionally. Without a healthy and available father, Rick had no model for manhood, no plan of action for how to be a healthy husband and father.

Every generation is the product of the previous three or four, and we live our lives based on the inherited and cultivated tendencies we got from someone else. Not a great idea! This is why self-examination, including studying the histories of those who preceded us, is so important and valuable to our healing and change.

Rick is honestly working on his stuff. He has been more regular in his meetings with his counselor. He has stopped drinking, but he is still suffering the consequences of it both physically and emotionally. He is "giving his mother a break" and endeavoring to understand how he ended up so angry and so needy of love and acceptance. Little by little, we pray that he and Misty can have a pleasant life and that their children, by observing the changes in their parents, can choose a better way, too.

MARIA

Abandonment occurs when a mother physically, emotionally or psychologically removes herself from her children. She does this by ending or ignoring her responsibility to parent her children, or ending her relationship with her children.

Peter Gerlach, MSW.

In an article on the website www.Livestrong.com professionals weigh in on the effects of abandonment:

Low Self-Esteem

Long-term effects of abandonment influence how a person feels about herself and her sense of self-worth. As a teenager or adult, coping mechanisms may be inadequate when managing painful situations, and a person with a history of abandonment may have difficulty relating with a spouse or partner.

Anxiety

Children aware they were abandoned may later show signs of anxiety while relating to caregivers or important people in their lives. Doris Landry, an author and educational expert in the field of international adoption, works with children who were abandoned as infants in China. Although they were adopted into loving families, the children still dealt with severe anxiety as manifested by difficulty separating from parents, sleep issues and controlling behavior.

Attachment

An abandoned child may have difficulty forming lasting bonds with others, particularly new caregivers. A child being cared for after abandonment may not attach with a new family and remain indifferent toward family members. He may have a lack of trust in others, fearing the departure of someone else important to him. By not allowing himself to bond with others, he rationalizes that he will not feel hurt again if he is rejected.

References:

- Child Welfare League of America: Baby Abandonment: Fact Sheet
- Rainbowkids: Mending a Broken Heart
- Gearingup: Nebraska Safe Haven Laws: Unintended Results
- Child Welfare Information Gateway: Child Neglect: A Guide for Intervention
- Focus Adolescent Services: Attachment and Attachment Disorders

Lately we have not heard much from Maria, but we do know this: Maria has backed down a great deal regarding her need to hold onto her mother through gifts and constant time with her, etc. She seldom worries that her mother will move off to another city.

Her relationship with her husband has improved as well. Sad, isn't it, that when a parent is missing in a child's life, that child grows up not knowing how to behave or react with other people.

Maria had a hard time connecting emotionally and even sexually with her husband, leaving him feeling abandoned and alone. Now, however, after gaining knowledge and beginning a program of self-examination and discovery, their marriage is improving, too.

Her husband, who grew up as the lost child in a large family, no longer feels quite so needy, alone, or unloved.

You know, anything worth doing takes time, effort and commitment. So it is with recovery. We will recover for the rest of our lives. As we often verbalize it, "We peel like an onion, one layer at a time. And sometimes we cry."

So as we look at who and what we came from; as we honestly admit to ourselves that our feelings, our thoughts, and our behaviors have been far from perfect; and as we confess those faults to ourselves and to another, including God, we begin to feel the weight of the world dropping off our backs. As we write our story in the process of doing either the *Binding the Wounds* or *The Journey* recovery program, and as we write letters of confession sharing how we felt at the time we were wounded and what effects that wound has had on our lives and the lives of others through us, relief comes. We begin to see that who we have been has not served us or others well, and we begin to see the truth of who God really designed us to be. Wow! What a difference!

MIKE and ALANA

In an extensive study performed and reported by Patricia Noller, Anita Blakeley-Smith and Susan Conway of the University of Queensland entitled "Comparison and Competition in Sibling and Twin Relationships: A Self-Evaluation Maintenance Perspective," the researchers summarize the main adult results of sibling comparison as:

- Downplaying the significance of one's performance

- Likelihood of continuing to evaluate and downplay one's performance

- Sibling relationship quality negatively impacted, without intervention or healing

Added to the above was Mike's continuing need to prove himself, his worth, and his value through his performance at work and at home. Included in the paper cited above, the authors cite the need to perform at home in order to please a marital partner, and Mike was definitely a classic case in this regard.

Mike and Alana have had some "ahas" and some life changes, too. Both are very gifted and talented individuals and experts in their fields.

Mike has had to look at how his need for attention and affirmation from his parents has orchestrated his behaviors. Workaholism often stems from the need to prove your worth and value to someone—to yourself, your parents, or others. Sometimes we work hard to try to prove to God that we are OK to save. The comparisons that went on between Mike and his sister were unfair, and to a degree, at least, they angered Mike. That anger gave him the adrenalin he needed to keep pushing on, working harder and longer hours to achieve an acceptable value of himself.

Unfortunately, doing this took him away from his God-given brain gift and forced him to struggle in a quadrant that was not his gift, and he began to suffer the consequences in relation to his children and to his own health. Not a good thing! Recently we reminded him of his need to be true to himself and to the gift that God has given him. He said, "Yea, you're right. I slow down and then, even before I recognize it, I am back to pushing again. Keep reminding me, OK?"

There is a law of the mind that is important for us to memorize. We should post it on our bathroom mirror, on the refrigerator, or maybe on our computer's desktop. It is:

"With every period of exhaustion, there is a corresponding period of depression, which goes to our weakest point."

Exhaustion is anything we do that taxes us physically, emotionally, or spiritually. Depression can be displayed in many ways. I would turn to withdrawal and tears, while Ron would tend to come out snipping at me or manufacturing something to create a fight about.

Think about how you get exhausted. What does it do to you, and how long do you let it happen before you recognize it and stop the behavior?

How do you behave when that exhaustion turns to depression? Do you withdraw, or do you lash out at others?

Is it worth staying on the merry-go-round or in the rat race? Is it worth damaging your health or destroying your relationships? We think not!

What do you do to make yourself feel better? A long, hot bath? Something creative like painting or knitting? Or do you turn to a self-destructive habit in order to stay above life's stressors?

ANOTHER LOOK

Recently I chatted with a woman whom I love. She is over-weight and is in what she terms a "loveless marriage." Due to the wounds of her childhood, she has allowed her parents' negative words to keep replaying in her mind, and as a result she has allowed herself to be, to a degree, dumbed down. As we talked, she shared her feelings, but with difficulty. You see, she had never really been allowed to express them as a child, while she endured the pain of her beginnings, so she "stuffed them down" and "kept getting bigger to hold them."

Finally she exploded in anger, which for her is a big deal! She let out all her anger and frustrations, and once they were out, she could think more clearly about her options. You can be sure I will be monitoring her progress and helping her as I can.

Alana does that, too. She makes believe that the world is her oyster and that all is well. She keeps herself very busy, as her husband Mike does, doing delightful projects; but both work and delightful projects take their toll. She keeps her house im-maculate! There is a place for everything, and everything is perfectly in its place. She is immaculately dressed whenever we see her, and her closet is filled with the wardrobe she needs to make herself look perfect. She, too, is stuffing emotions, but in her case into her closet!

We understand that the need for acceptance and perfection has subsided some in this couple, and we pray that, as they con-tinue their journey of recovery, the need to be filled with ac-complishments will be dispelled and instead they will be com-pletely filled with God's love and grace.

When all we have looked at in these chapters can cause us to let go of the harmful effects of the past in a process of healing and recovery, we, too, just like Ron and Sam, can be free!

Chapter Twelve

Wrapping It Up

The purpose of this book was to demonstrate, through science and the lives of particular individuals, just how catastrophic childhood abuse can be to the lives of victims, and what can be done about it. Wounds they've received have both the history and the potential of perverting the thinking, feeling and behaviors of those who endure them.

While many would love to believe that religion and spiritual practice alone can transform a life, the reality is that very few of the wounded can comprehend and obtain emotional life change by attending church or reading the Bible or other inspired writings.

In Ron's case, it was the embrace that he'd been missing all his life that got him to do more than attend church just to intimidate the preacher. It was Haswell's inclusion of him, and calling him "Son," that got his attention and made him willing not only to attend services but to begin to listen to the truth. Even then, while he was still incarcerated, Ron was enticed by the desire for acceptance; and, in the process, he received the logic of Biblical truth. Once out of prison, it was easy for him to slip back to responding to life the same way he had before prison.

Agreeing to the doctrines of a denomination, and even being baptized as Jesus was, does not change one's memories; and Ron's were filled with the pain of rejection, especially from his mother. When he married Nancy and placed her in the mother role, his attitudes and behaviors toward her were a reflection of his feelings about his mother.

You might say, "Well, Sam was converted by the Bible and the lessons in the correspondence course." But what did it take for Sam, a man headed for death row in prison, to give any attention at all to the claims of the Gospel of Jesus Christ? It took the persistence of two ordinary men from a local church who demonstrated a kind of love and caring that he had never known. It took the sacrifice of a little boy who gave up his new Bible to a convict, and it took the intervention of the Holy Spirit. In actuality, responding to any kind of plea from God to an individual always takes the intervention of the Holy Spirit.

In Ron's life, it took Leonard Haswell's response to a call for ministry to prisoners; it took the Spirit urging Haswell to put his arm around Ron and call him "Son." It required the softening of Ron's heart by the working of the Spirit upon him so that he would even consider God. Neither individual knew at the time that this Spirit, this demonstrated caring, could begin a work in Ron that would later include identification of and recovery from the deep wounds of rejection and neglect. Intellectual knowledge and ascent to the Gospel alone did not transform Ron's life.

It soon became evident after his release from prison that his work had only just begun. You see, life transformation, or recovery, is the work of a lifetime. It's called sanctification. It is the process of becoming whole and holy. One may come to Christ, prostrate himself at the foot of the cross, and even feel sorrow for his sins, but that does not change his memories—his thoughts and feelings. Oh, it may change his behaviors temporarily, but old habits die hard.

Look at the Apostle Paul, the great teacher and revivalist of the New Testament. Even late in his career, he was complaining about the good he should do that he didn't and the evil he shouldn't do that he did. His Damascus Road experience got his attention all right, and it even changed his focus and his goals, but it did not change the memories that made him the often harsh and abrasive champion for Christ.

It wasn't until Ron was out of prison, with all of life's temptations readily available to him, that his experience with the Lord began to be less important and less satisfying of his need for survival. He thought that succumbing to these temptations would bring him all the attention, affection, caring, and pain relief that he wasn't getting from his wife. But enough was not enough.

Let's face it. No human being alive can fill the emptiness in the heart of another. That's just not possible. It is true that God can fill that need—that longing for intimacy that should have been experienced in the womb and in the cradle. But complete trust in one you cannot see does not come easy, especially when, in your experience, no one is trustworthy. Trust should have been developed during the first 18 months of life, and if it wasn't, it develops as mistrust.

Erickson, a psychologist who practiced and researched years ago, created what is called Erickson's Life Span. In it we see that the development of trust comes first in the life of an infant. Looking at the following chart to find what should be developed and when, we can discover a great deal about ourselves.

The first developmental step is trust vs. mistrust. The most significant relationship during that time is with one's mother. Her care, presence, and feeding of the child contribute to this development. During that period the question is answered, positively or negatively, "Can I trust the world?" If trust is developed, hope is the virtue that comes as a bonus.

In the chart that follows, you will see the ages at which certain developments should occur, the virtues that result from these developments, the developments themselves, the significant relationships involved with the developments, the questions that we unknowingly ask ourselves during these phases, and examples of each developmental accomplishment—or what should be accomplished. Go through the chart carefully to honestly determine at what stage of development you find yourself.

Approx. Age	Virtues	Development	Significant Relationship	Existential Question	Examples
birth-1 yr.	Hope	Basic Trust vs. Mistrust	Mother	Can I Trust the World?	Feeding, Abandonment
2–3 yrs	Will	Autonomy vs. Shame and Doubt	Parents	Is It Okay To Be Me?	Toilet Training, Clothing Themselves
3–5 yrs		Initiative vs. Guilt	Family	Is It Okay For Me To Do, Move and Act?	Exploring, Using Tools or Making Art
6–12 yrs	Capable	Industry vs. Inferiority	Neighbors, School	Can I Make It In The World Of People And Things?	School, Sports
13–18 yrs	Fidelity	Identity vs. Role Confusion	Peers, Role Model	Who Am I? What Can I Be?	Social Relationships
18-40 yrs (young adulthood)	Love	Intimacy vs. Isolation	Friends, Partners	Can I Love?	Romantic Relationships
40-65 yrs (middle adulthood)	Care	Generativity vs. Stagnation	Household, Workmates	Can I Make My Life Count?	Work Parenthood
65-death (old age)	Wise	Ego Integrity vs. Despair	Mankind, My Kind	Is It Okay To Have Been Me?	Reflection on Life

Each step in the process of development builds upon the other. If trust is developed, then the development of autonomy or self-government is the next step. If we can develop this step, then will and decision making happen in us.

If we miss a step, especially step one, then it is difficult to get to step two.

If steps one and two do not develop, how easy is it to develop initiative—step three?

Look at all of these stages and ask yourself how well you have accomplished them. Are you stuck back at 12-18 months of age and can't trust anyone, including God? When you are absolutely honest with yourself, you just might find yourself in need of climbing the steps to adult maturity.

Here is another list of the results of childhood wounds on adult behaviors. This look in the mirror might not be any easier than the previous chart, but it is a major help in telling ourselves the truth. **Which of the items on this list are behaviors you deal with or have dealt with in the past?**

- Conforming to others' expectations for acceptance

- Difficulty making proper decisions; decisions are made by default or are based on childish, self-centered wants

- Forming co-dependent relationships; your partner becomes your parent, or "the rocks in your head fit the holes in mine"

- Refusing to be held accountable, but blaming everyone else and holding others accountable; these are survival behaviors

- Having little or no self-confidence (but may appear arrogant to others)

- Communicating by screaming, pouting, using extremes (you always, you never), refusing to speak, having nothing to say

- Isolating; hiding in substances, books, TV, reading, sleep, or even religion

- Trouble managing anger

- Being overly possessive of partner, children, or friends

- Being financially unstable or irresponsible

- Little or no discernment; appearing to understand others with no understanding of oneself

- Exaggerated sexual feelings and behaviors; sexual addiction or being overly driven (multiple partners, masturbation, demanding sex frequently)

- Difficulty bonding with another adult

- Feeling hostile, anxious, depressed, insecure, inhibited, inferior, indifferent, withdrawn, overly compliant, or submissive to an extreme

The Bible speaks about maturity in the book of Ephesians. It counsels us to no longer be infants tossed about by every wind, but to "grow up" into maturity. It even tells us how we get there and what maturity looks like.

> *. . . that we should no longer be children, tossed to and fro and carried about . . . but speaking the truth in love, grow up in all things into Him who is the head—Christ.*

Ephesians 4: 12-13.

> *Let all bitterness, wrath, anger, clamor and evil speaking be put away from you, with all malice. And be kind to one another, tender-hearted, forgiving one another, even as God in Christ forgave you.*

Ibid. Verses 31 and 32.

ANOTHER LOOK AT SAM

Sam recognized quite early in life that he wasn't going to get the things he needed—things like love, acceptance, nurturing, safety, and pleasure—so, in order to survive, he took those things that he thought would make him happy. This led him to a short life of crime and ultimately to his death.

Ron's story is similar. When children don't get what they need, they often turn to shiny, pretty things to make them happy. So said Dr. John Bowlby, a British psychologist and the father of Attachment Theory. Bowlby's theory of attachment suggests that children come into the world biologically pre-programmed to form attachments with others, because this will help them to survive. The basis of his theory is:

1. A child has an innate (inborn) need to attach to one main attachment figure.

2. A child should receive the continuous care of this single most important attachment figure for approximately the first two years of life.

3. The long-term consequences of maternal deprivation might include the following:

   - delinquency

   - reduced intelligence

   - increased aggression

   - depression

   - affectionless psychopathy

   Affectionless psychopathy is an inability to show affection or concern for others. Such individuals act on impulse with little regard for the consequences of their actions.

4. The child's attachment relationship with their primary care-giver leads to the development of an **internal working model**.

As we look back on the stories of Ron, Sam, Ricky, and Maria, we see this pattern of detachment occurring and the subsequent difficulty of these four individuals in forming secure attachments in adulthood. How could we expect them to form attachments with God, whom they cannot see, hear or touch?

It is most interesting that God knew that we could be deprived of the intimacy that He planned we would have with our birth parents, and that is why he calls Himself "Father." He is the ideal replacement for both mother and father, as he fulfills the roles of provider, protector and priest—a father's duty to his children—and also has the qualities of a mother—compassionate, concerned and caregiver. He is, in fact, everything we as mature adults need not only to survive, but to thrive.

He is the ultimate altruistic parent who empathizes with our condition and offers to us not only love, peace and joy, but also an eternity to spend with every quality we missed in childhood.

The Bible tells us that He knows our frame, He knew us before we were formed in our mother's womb, and he knows the pain we carry and longs to be intimately involved in our process of being relieved from its devastating effects.

He encourages us to examine ourselves, to look inside at our motives, our thoughts, and our feelings, and, even unknowingly, to allow His power to fill us as we process through the pain we have received and experienced.

People hurt! Their hurt causes them to hurt themselves and others. Most people have been dealt an unfortunate hand: a physical disease, a negative disposition, a tendency toward anger and aggression, or any of the addictions. But we are not stuck with that hand! In actuality, looking at those who came before us in our gene pool assists us in understanding some of the thoughts, feelings and behaviors that we have today. That's why contemplating and investigating our personal histories is so beneficial.

Often the physical and mental condition and the habits of parents are passed on to their offspring. Whenever the habits of the parents are contrary to physical law, the injury they have experienced will be repeated in future generations.

Remember, both positive and negative habits can be passed down through many generations.

The longing in Jesus' heart to relieve that pain, emotionally and physically, is demonstrated in the story of the paralytic who lay beside the pool of Bethesda. For 38 long years he had languished there, waiting for help from someone, but none came—until Jesus. As he stood beside the man who lay in his filth and desperation, Jesus asked him if he wanted to be healed. The amazing response Jesus received is often the response we give ourselves, each other, and even God.

"Yea, but"—a famous expression in our vocabulary, and apparently in Jesus' day too. And then the excuses poured out of him: "No one is here to help me when the waters move, others get to the water before I can. I'm paralyzed, can't you see?"

Jesus heard his excuses, just as he hears ours—we hurting individuals of today. And Jesus said to the paralyzed man, "Get up!" The Bible does not record that Jesus lifted him, shoved him into the pool, or got someone else to do it. He just said, "Get up!"

The paralytic just needed enough faith to believe that he could do it. Jesus supplied that faith for him.

Ron didn't have faith either, but Haswell did, and so did all the male mentors who came after Haswell: Joe Damazo, the Milwaukee pastor who took Ron "under his wing" the day he came out of prison and for months afterward, and who to this day remains a loyal encourager; Jim Hallas, Nancy's dad, who finally had a son and treated him as such; and Ralph Larson, who was a guide and mentor during Ron's college years and up until his death.

Sam was fatherless and was suffering the torment of the damned when two men preached a sermon about Christ's love and acceptance. They were not fearful of the convicted murderer; rather, they boldly approached and gave him a bit of their faith so that Sam could respond to the Holy Spirit's call on his life. Sam had the correspondence school at Faith For Today and the teachers who faithfully corresponded with him. And then Sam had Pastor William A. Fagal, who actually was with him at the time of his death, offering a bit of his faith to see Sam through.

And Ricky has Ron—a guy who has been where Rick is, knows full well Rick's pain, and walks alongside him offering hope and courage for his journey from darkness into the full light of God's grace and mercy. In his angst that resulted from his beginning, Rick steals things too—the joy from his wife and children that they should be experiencing in life. Rick still blames God for not rescuing him from a desperate mother, an angry and absent father, two stepbrothers who raped him, and the torment he has endured since. But we see Rick as a spiritual and emotional giant—perhaps not yet, but Ron will continue to be his mentor until the time comes when he is able to transfer his dependence and counsel onto God.

You might say, "That's a whole lot of God-speak! Since I don't have that much faith, is healing possible for me?" And the answer would be that science has proven that we can change the genes we've inherited. We can even change illness in our bodies through a change of habit and state of mind. The idle can choose activity in order to re-wire some of the needed neurons in the brain, creating an increase in circulation and health. Those who are overweight can cut out sugar and its detrimental effects, slowing down the firestorm in the body that it creates and sending diabetes and cardiovascular illness packing. And when they begin to exercise, their blood pressure and other body systems will improve.

The same is true for our emotional well-being. Identifying and processing those inherited tendencies that have come down the line to you, and that you've cultivated and perhaps even exaggerated, can transform your emotional life and even your thoughts and feelings. Many scientists who specialize in genetics are saying that your perceptions change your genes. You do not have to be controlled by what came down to you! A simple change in perception, which will come as you process through your wounds, will change your genes. You do not have to remain the product of them! As we change, our perceptions change. As our perceptions change, the way we view God changes also.

In Appendix I you will find the form for the letter we have talked about: *A Letter for Healing.* Make sure that you don't spare your words. Write out your memories and the feelings your wound has produced in detail. Make sure that you identify all of the detrimental effects that the wound you received has had on you. The hand will write what the mouth cannot speak.

Share your story and your progress with others. If you can find a group of folks who are of the same gender as yourself, form a group and support each other through your journey. If you can, use the process already written in either *The Journey* or *Binding the Wounds.* Both programs are available for purchase by sending an e-mail to rockeys@itsfixable.com with your request for information. Thousands around the world have been using these programs with amazing results!

Perhaps your heart is failing you for fear of what is in it, and you don't know how to get rid of the old stuff that still haunts you. Whether you are a criminal, a person who feels defeated, lonely, or depressed, an angry man, or a hopeless teen, the tools for your healing are here for you in this book. Find a person who will walk alongside you and who has enough faith in God for your positive changes. He or she should be a listening ear, a partner in recovery. They should be at least partially healed themselves and have their focus and perception changed, because, believe it or not, our perceptions change our genes!

Each one is to be to the wounded as Jesus was to the paralytic— offer enough faith, and the proper knowledge, so the wounded can get up! That begins the perception alteration process, and God promises to supply the power.

Regardless of where you are, what you feel, and what you may have done, God has His hand on you. You are his priceless son or daughter for whom He gave the life of His Son. Be teachable, follow what you've read about recovery, and work through the pain of your past. God has promised to walk alongside you. Psalm 23 offers that hope. He restores your soul and leads you down the path of righteousness; He walks through the valley of the shadow of death with you so that you have to fear no evil; He comforts you, and He promises that goodness and mercy will follow you all the days of your life, and that you will live in the house of the Lord forever. Let this be your comfort as you begin to process through your healing. Our prayers will accompany you!

Appendix I

A Letter For Healing

Dear_____ ;

The purpose of this letter is to share with you the pain I received as the result of:

I want you to know that I appreciate:

I want to share with you the pain I have carried as a result of:

The effect on my life of the damage done to me has been:

My goals and plans for the future include:

This letter is being written as a part of my healing process. It is to empty myself of the _____ that I have felt toward you since _____ .

You may want to start this letter on lined 8" x 11½" paper so that you can write far more than this space allows. Use this outline for every wound and every individual you feel has wounded you. Be sure you write until you have nothing more to say.

When you have finished writing a letter, share it with someone you trust, reading aloud to that person. Then feel free to shred it, burn it, or keep it in a locked place. Then ask God to pour His forgiveness into you for that offender.

Appendix II

What Is The ACE Study?

The ACE Study is ongoing collaborative research between the Centers for Disease Control and Prevention in Atlanta, GA, and Kaiser Permanente in San Diego, CA.

The Co-principal Investigators of The Study are Robert F. Anda, MD, MS, with the CDC; and Vincent J. Felitti, MD, with Kaiser Permanente.

Over 17,000 Kaiser patients participating in routine health screening volunteered to participate in The Study. Data resulting from their participation continues to be analyzed; it reveals staggering proof of the health, social, and economic risks that result from childhood trauma.

The Centers for Disease Control and Prevention provides access to the peer-reviewed publications resulting from The ACE Study.

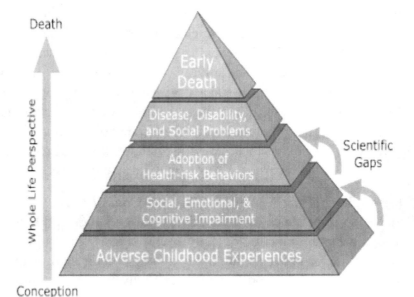

The Adverse Childhood Experiences Study is an outgrowth of observations we made in the mid 1980s in an obesity program that had a high dropout rate. The first of many unexpected discoveries was that the majority of the dropouts actually were successfully losing weight. Accidentally and to our surprise, we learned from detailed life interviews of 286 such individuals that childhood sexual abuse was remarkably common and, if present, always antedated the onset of their obesity. No one previously had sought this kind of medical information from them but many patients spoke of their conscious awareness of an association between abuse and obesity. Some told of instances where they had brought up their history of abuse only to have the information rejected by a physician as being in the distant past and hence of no relevance to current problems.

The counterintuitive aspect was that, for many people, obesity was not their problem; it was their protective *solution* to problems that previously had never been acknowledged to anyone. An early insight was the remark of a woman who was raped at age twenty-three and gained 105 pounds in the year subsequent: "Overweight is overlooked and that's the way I need to be." The contrast was striking between this statement and her desire to lose weight. Similarly, two men who were guards at the State Penitentiary became anxious after each losing over one hundred pounds. They said that they felt much safer going to work looking larger than life rather than normal size. In general, we found the simultaneous presence of strong opposing forces to be common in our obese patients. Many were driving with one foot on the brakes and one on the gas, wanting to lose weight but fearful of the change in social and sexual expectations that would be brought about by major weight loss.

Researchers at the Centers for Disease Control (CDC) recognized the importance of these clinical observations and helped design a large, epidemiologically sound study that would provide definitive proof of our findings and of their significance. The Adverse Childhood Experiences Study was carried out in

Kaiser Permanente's Department of Preventive Medicine in San Diego. This was an ideal setting because for many years we had carried out detailed biomedical, psychological, and social (biopsychosocial) evaluations of over 58,000 adult Kaiser Health Plan members a year. Moreover, the patients were from a typical middle class American population. We asked 26,000 consecutive adults coming through the Department if they would be interested in helping us understand how childhood events might affect adult health status. Seventy-one percent agreed.

We asked these volunteers to help us study eight categories of childhood abuse and household dysfunction. The abuse categories were: recurrent physical abuse, recurrent severe emotional abuse, and contact sexual abuse. The five categories of household dysfunction were: growing up in a household where someone was in prison; where the mother was treated violently; with an alcoholic or a drug user; where someone was chronically depressed, mentally ill, or suicidal; and where at least one biological parent was lost to the patient during childhood—regardless of cause. An individual exposed to none of the categories had an ACE Score of 0; an individual exposed to any four had an ACE Score of 4, etc. In addition, a prospective arm of the Study is following the cohort for at least 5 years to compare distant childhood experiences against current Emergency Department use, doctor office visits, medication costs, hospitalization, and death.

Dr. Anda, my co-principal investigator at CDC, designed with great skill the massive data management and retrospective and prospective components of the Study. Because the average participant was 57 years old, we actually were measuring the effect of childhood experiences on adult health status a half-century later. The full text of our initial report is at http://www.meddevel.com/site.mash?left=/library.exe&m1=4& m2=1&right=/library.exe&action=search_form&search.mode= simple&site=AJPM&jcode=AMEPRE.

Our two most important findings are that these adverse child-hood experiences: **are vastly more common than recognized or acknowledged and have a powerful relation to adult health a half-century later.**

This combination makes them important to the nation's health and to medical practice. Slightly more than half of our middle-class population of Kaiser members experienced one or more of the categories of adverse childhood experience that we studied. One in four were exposed to two categories of adverse experi-ence; one in 16 were exposed to four categories.

Given an exposure to one category, there is 80% likelihood of exposure to another category. Of course, all this is well shielded by social taboos against seeking or obtaining this kind of information. Furthermore, one may miss the forest for the trees if one studies the categories individually. They do not oc-cur in isolation; for instance, a child does not grow up with an alcoholic parent or with domestic violence in an otherwise supportive and well-functioning household. The question to ask is: How will these childhood experiences play out decades later in a doctor's office? To study that, we will categorize out-comes into organic disease and emotional disorder.

Organic disease

We shall first look at the relationship of adverse childhood ex-periences to smoking. Smoking underlies some of the most important causes of death in America; there has been a strong public health effort to eradicate smoking in California. In spite of initial success in significantly reducing the number of smok-ers, there has been no further net decrease in recent years al-though the efforts against smoking have continued. Because of this, smoking in the face of California's strong social pressures against it is often attributed to 'addiction.' The usual concept of tobacco addiction implies that it is attributable to characteris-tics that are intrinsic within the molecular structure of nicotine.

However, we found that the higher the ACE Score, the greater the likelihood of current smoking. In other words, current smoking is strongly related in a progressive dose-response manner to what happened decades ago in childhood. Finding 'addiction' attributable to characteristics that are intrinsic in early life experiences challenges the conventional concept of addiction. The psychoactive benefits of nicotine are well established in the medical literature although they are little remembered. Are smoking and its related diseases the result of self-treatment of concealed problems that occurred in childhood?

ACE Score vs. Smoking

Chronic obstructive pulmonary disease (COPD) also has a strong relationship to the ACE Score, as does the early onset of regular smoking. A person with an ACE Score of 4 is 260% more likely to have COPD than is a person with an ACE Score of 0. This relationship has the same graded, dose-response effect that is present for *all* the associations we found. Moreover, all the relationships presented here have a p value of .001 or stronger.

ACE Score vs. COPD

When we compared hepatitis in ACE Score 0 patients with hepatitis in ACE Score 4 patients, there was a 240% increase in prevalence. A progressive dose response effect was present with every increase in the ACE Score. Similarly, with regard to sexually transmitted disease, comparison of the adjusted odds ratio for sexually transmitted disease in these same two groups showed a 250% increase at ACE Score 4 compared to ACE Score 0.

In the United States, intravenous drug use is a major public health problem with which little progress has been made. It is widely recognized as a cause of several life-threatening diseases. We found that the relationship of iv drug use to adverse childhood experiences is powerful and graded at every step; it provides a perfect dose-response curve.

ACE Score vs. Intravenous Drug Use

In Epidemiology, these results are almost unique in their magnitude. For example, a male child with an ACE Score of 6 has a 4,600% increase in the likelihood of later becoming an iv drug user when compared to a male child with an ACE Score of 0. Since no one injects heroin to get endocarditis or AIDS, why *is* it used? Might heroin be used for the relief of profound anguish dating back to childhood experiences? Might its psychoactive effects be the best coping device that an individual can find? Is intravenous drug use properly viewed as a personal *solution* to problems that are well concealed by social niceties and taboo? If so, is intravenous drug use a public health problem or a personal solution? Is it both? How often are public health problems personal solutions? Is drug abuse self-destructive or is it a desperate attempt at self-healing, albeit while accepting a significant future risk? This is an important point because primary prevention is far more difficult than anticipated. Is this because non-recognition of the *benefits* of health risk behaviors leads them to be viewed as irrational and as solely having damaging consequences? Does this major oversight leave us speaking in platitudes instead of understanding the causal basis of some of our intractable public health problems?

Emotional disorders

When we looked at purely emotional outcomes like self-defined current depression or self-reported suicide attempts, we find equally powerful effects. For instance, we found that an individual with an ACE Score of 4 or more was 460% more likely to be suffering from depression than an individual with an ACE Score of 0. Should one doubt the reliability of this, we found that there was a 1,220% increase in attempted suicide between these two groups. At higher ACE Scores, the prevalence of attempted suicide increases 30-51fold (3,000-5,100%)! Our article describing this staggering effect was published in a recent issue of the Journal of the American Medical Association.

Overall, using the technique of population attributable risk, we found that between two-thirds and 80% of all attempted suicides could be attributed to adverse childhood experiences.

ACE Score vs. Attempted Suicide

In addition to these examples, we found many other measures of adult health have a strong, graded relationship to what happened in childhood: heart disease, fractures, diabetes, obesity, unintended pregnancy sexually transmitted diseases, and alcoholism were more frequent. Occupational health and job performance worsened progressively as the ACE Score increased. Some of these results are yet to be published, as is all the data from the prospective arm of the Study that will relate adverse childhood experiences to medical care costs, disease, and death a half-century later.

Clearly, we have shown that adverse childhood experiences are common, destructive, and have an effect that often lasts for a lifetime. They are the most important determinant of the health and well-being of our nation. Unfortunately, these problems are painful to recognize and difficult to deal with. Most physicians would far rather deal with traditional organic disease. Certainly, it is easier to do so, but that approach also leads to troubling treatment failures and the frustration of expensive diagnostic quandaries where everything is ruled out but nothing is ruled in.

Our usual approach to many adult chronic diseases reminds one of the relationship of smoke to fire. For a person unfamiliar with fires, it would initially be tempting to treat the smoke because that is the most visible aspect of the problem. Fortunately, fire departments learned long ago to distinguish cause from effect; else, they would carry fans rather than water hoses to their work. What we have learned in the ACE Study represents the underlying fire in medical practice where we often treat symptoms rather than underlying causes.

Vincent J. Felitti, MD 6 German ACE article.

If the treatment implications of what we found in the ACE Study are far-reaching, the prevention aspects are positively daunting. The very nature of the material is such as to make one uncomfortable. Why would one want to leave the relative comfort of traditional organic disease and enter this area of threatening uncertainty that none of us has been trained to deal with? And yet, literally as I am writing these words, I am interrupted to consult on a 70-yearold woman who is diabetic and hypertensive. The initial description given to me left out the fact that she is morbidly obese (one doesn't go out of one's way to identify what one can't handle). Review of her chart shows her to be chronically depressed, never married, and, because we routinely ask the question of 58,000 adults a year, to have been raped by her older brother six decades ago when she was ten. That brother molested her sister who is said also to be leading a troubled life.

We found that 22% of our Kaiser members were sexually abused as children. How does that Affect a person later in life? How does it show up in the doctor's office? What does it mean that sexual abuse is never spoken of? Most of us initially are uncomfortable about obtaining or using such information; therefore we find it useful routinely to pose such questions to all patients by questionnaire. Our Yes response rates are quite high as the ACE Study indicates. We then ask patients acknowledging such experience, "*How did that affect you later in life?*" This question is easy to ask and is neither judgmental nor threatening to hear. It works well and you should remember to use it. It typically provides profoundly important information, and does so concisely. It often gives one a clear idea where to go with treatment.

What then is this woman's diagnosis? Is she just another hypertensive, diabetic old woman or is there more to the practice of medicine? Here is the way we conceptualized her problems:

Childhood sexual abuse

Chronic depression

Morbid obesity

Diabetes mellitus

Hypertension

Hyperlipidemia

Coronary artery disease

Macular degeneration

Psoriasis

This is not a comfortable diagnostic formulation because it points out that our attention is typically focused on tertiary consequences, far downstream. It reveals that the primary issues are well protected by social convention and taboo. It points out that we physicians have limited ourselves to the smallest part of the problem, that part where we are comfortable as mere prescribers of medication. Which diagnostic choice shall we make? Who shall make it? And, if not now, when?

References

1. Felitti VJ, Anda RF, Nordenberg D, Williamson DF, Spitz AM, Edwards V, Koss MP, et al JS. The relationship of adult health status to childhood abuse and household dysfunction. American Journal of Preventive Medicine. 1998;14:245-258.

2. Foege WH. Adverse childhood experiences: A public health perspective (editorial). American Journal of Preventive Medicine. 1998;14:354-355.

3. Weiss JS, Wagner SH. What explains the negative consequences of adverse childhood experiences on adult health? Insights from cognitive and neuroscience research (editorial). American Journal of Preventive Medicine. 1998;14:356-360.

4. Anda RF, Croft JB, Felitti VJ, Nordenberg D, Giles WH, Williamson DF, et al. Adverse childhood experiences and smoking during adolescence and adulthood. Journal of the American Medical Association. 1999; 282:1652-1658.

5. Dube SR, Anda RF, Felitti VJ, Chapman DP, Williamson DF, Giles WH. Childhood Abuse, Household Dysfunction, and the Risk of Attempted Suicide Throughout the Lifespan. JAMA 2001; 286: 3089-3096.

6. Dietz PM, Spitz AM, Anda RF, et al. Unintended pregnancy among adult women exposed to abuse or household dysfunction during their childhood. Journal of the American Medical Association. 1999;282:1359-1364.

7. Hillis SD, Anda RF, Felitti VJ, Nordenberg D, Marchbanks PA. Adverse childhood experiences and sexually transmitted diseases in men and women: a retrospective study. Pediatrics 2000 106(1):E11.

Bibliography

Dennis A. Balcom, The Journal of Men's Studies, *Absent Fathers: Effects on Abandoned Sons,* March 22, 1998.

John Bowlby, *Loss, Sadness and Depression,* New York: Vintage Publishing, 1998.

Ron and Nancy Rockey, *Belonging,* Boise, Idaho: Pacific Press, 1998.

Bruce D. Perry, *Born to Love,* Harper Collins Publishers, New York, 2010.

William A. Fagal, *By God's Grace, Sam,* Washington D.C.: Review and Herald Publishing Association, 1958.

Ron and Nancy Rockey, *Chosen,* Boise, Idaho: Pacific Press, 2001.

Joan McCord, Encyclopedia of Crime and Justice. Article entitled: *Family Relationships and Crime,* USA: MacMillian Reference, 2002.

Mark R. Leary, *Interpersonal Rejection,* New York: Oxford University Press, 2001.

Ronald P. Rohner, Abdul Khaleque, David E. Cournoyer, *Introduction to Parental Acceptance and Rejection Theory, Methods, Evidence and Implications,* University of Connecticut's Center for the Study of Parental Acceptance and Rejection, 2012.

John Bowlby, *Maternal Care and Mental Health,* New York: Scocken Books, 1966.

Genevieve Van Wyden, *Mother Abandonment The Effects On the Child* http://www.livestrong.com/article/159897.

H.J. Eysenck et al., "PersonalityType, Smoking Habit and their Interaction as Predictors of Cancer and Coronary Disease." *Personality and Individual Difference* 9 (2) (1988): 479-495; H. Eysneck, *British Journal of Medical Psychology 61 (pt.1) 1988.*

David Perlmutter and Alberto Villoldo, *Power Up Your Brain,* New York City, N.Y., Hay House, Inc., 2011.

Thomas Verny, *Pre-Parenting,* New York: Simon and Schuster, 2002.

Jim Hopper, *Sexual abuse of Males, Prevalence, Possible Lasting Effects and Resources,* www.jimhopper.com, 2012.

Bruce D. Perryand Maia Szalavitz, *The Boy Who Was Raised As A Dog,* New York: Basic Books, 2008.

Alice Miller, *The Drama of Being A Child,* London, UK: Virago Press, 1987.

Vlad Tarko, *The Psychological Difficulties of Orphans,* Softpedia.com, 2006.

John Joseph Evoy, *The Rejected,* University Park, Pa.: The Pennsylvania State University Press, 1981.

Dr. Dan B. Allender, *The Wounded Heart,* Colorado Springs, CO.: Navpress, 1995.

Sheldon Glueck and Eleanor T. Glueck, "Unraveling Juvenile Delinquency." New York: Commonwealth Fund, 1950.

Other Books/Programs by Ron and Nancy Rockey

BOOKS

Belonging
Overcoming Rejection and Discovering the Freedom of Acceptance

Betrayed
Surviving a Marital Affair and Keeping the Marriage Intact

Chosen
God's Relentless Pursuit of His Wandering Child

Heart Connection
Science Uncovers the Secrets of True Intimacy

Shadows of Acceptance
Understanding the Illusion

RECOVERY PROGRAMS

Binding the Wounds
22-session program with videos and workbook

The Journey
40-session program in 4 segments with video, chapters and workbook

Created For Success
Program for couples

Journey to Nai
13-session program for teens

CPSIA information can be obtained at www.ICGtesting.com
Printed in the USA
LVOW06s0322110913

351806LV00002B/7/P